ATONEMENT, CHRISTOLOGY AND THE TRINITY

Vincent Brümmer is a philosopher of religion who takes systematic theology seriously. In his new book he uses his philosophical acumen to elucidate central topics of Christian doctrine: the Atonement, Christology, and the Trinity. For him they are not mere theological constructions but have their meaning and function in the context of the believer's search for ultimate happiness. There is much to be learned from his clear and careful philosophical reworking of classical views of Reformed theology. New and controversial is the idea of a 'matrix of faith' by which Christians claim to attain ultimate happiness and which Brümmer believes can be defended not only within the Christian, but also the Jewish and Islamic traditions. This will no doubt provoke discussion, and it should.
　　　　　　　　　– Professor Dr Ingolf Ulrich Dalferth, University of Zurich

Professor Vincent Brummer writes as an established philosopher of religion who places his philosophical expertise at the service of theology. Here he builds on his earlier work on the non-manipulative nature of true love, expounds the work of Christ as God's own act, and presses the logical entailments of language about atonement and the Trinity. Whether or not readers endorse all of his conclusions, his arguments are to be reckoned with and incisive observations and rigorous logic pose questions that need to be addressed. This is a challenging resource for ongoing debate in this area.
　　　　　　　　　– Anthony C. Thiselton, Emeritus Professor, University of Nottingham;
　　　　　　　　　Research Professor, Chester University College; and Canon Theologian,
　　　　　　　　　Leicester Cathedral and Southwell Minster

For many believers today the doctrines of Atonement, Christology and the Trinity seem like puzzling constructions produced by academic theologians. They are cast in unintelligible forms of thought derived from Platonism or from feudal society, and for many their existential relevance for life today remains unclear.

This book introduces these doctrines and proposes a reinterpretation in the light of the claim of many Christian mystics that ultimate happiness is to be found in enjoying the loving fellowship of God. This claim is a 'matrix of faith' in terms of which these doctrines are shown to be relevant for the life of faith of believers today. Furthermore, since this matrix can be defended within all three Abrahamic traditions, Judaism, Christianity and Islam, the proposed understanding of these doctrines can also contribute usefully to the necessary dialogue between these traditions in a globalized world.

Atonement, Christology and the Trinity

Making Sense of Christian Doctrine

VINCENT BRÜMMER
University of Utrecht, The Netherlands

ASHGATE

Published by
Ashgate Publishing Limited
Gower House, Croft Road
Aldershot, Hampshire
GU11 3HR
England

Ashgate Publishing Company
Suite 420
101 Cherry Street
Burlington, VT 05401–4405
USA

Ashgate website: http//www.ashgate.com

British Library Cataloguing in Publication Data
Brümmer, Vincent
  Atonement, Christology and the Trinity : making sense of
  Christian doctrine
  1. Jesus Christ – Person and offices 2. Theology, Doctrinal
  3. Atonement 4. Trinity
  I. Title
  230

Library of Congress Cataloging-in-Publication Data
Brümmer, Vincent
  Atonement, Christology, and the Trinity: making sense of Christian doctrine /
  Vincent Brümmer. – 1st ed.
     p. cm.
  Includes bibliographical references and index.
  ISBN 0–7546–5225–4 (hardccover : alk. paper) – ISBN 0–7546–5230–0 (pbk. : alk.
  paper) 1. Atonement. 2. Jesus Christ – Person and offices. 3. Trinity. I. Title.

  BT265.3.B78 2004
  230–dc22

2004014034

ISBN 0 7546 5230 0 (PBK)
ISBN 0 7546 5225 4 (HBK)

This book is printed on acid-free paper

Typeset in Times Roman by IML Typographers, Birkenhead, Merseyside

Printed in Great Britain by MPG Books Ltd. Bodmin

Contents

Acknowledgements

I would like to thank a number of friends and colleagues for reading the manuscript of this book and making some valuable suggestions for improving my argument and clarifying my ideas. First I would like to thank Professor David Brown from Durham for his friendly comments. I appreciate these especially since his approach to the issues discussed here is in many ways very different from mine. Secondly I am very grateful to Professor Roel van den Broek, my colleague for patristics in Utrecht, for checking my treatment of the Church Fathers and making sure that I have not misunderstood them. Thirdly I would like to thank Dr Saeid Edeladnejad from Tehran and Professor Ghasem Kakaie from Shiraz for going through my manuscript and making some very valuable comments from a Moslem point of view. I am also most grateful to Ghasem Kakaie for his kind invitation to run a graduate seminar on this book at Shiraz University during the first week of Ramadan in October 2004. The enthusiastic response of his students confirmed my claim that what I call the 'matrix of faith' is not only fundamental to the Christian tradition but could also very well be defended within an Islamic context. Finally I would like to thank Agneta Schreurs and the Scheurs family for permission to use the painting of Christ with the crown of thorns by Jaap Schreurs (1913–83) on the cover of this book. This painting provides a perfect expression of what in this book I call the 'price of forgiveness'.

PART 1
PROLOGUE

PART I
PROLOGUE

CHAPTER 1

The Intelligibility of Christian Doctrine

Mysteries and Puzzles

> Whosoever will be saved: before all things it is necessary that he hold the Catholic Faith ... And the Catholic Faith is this: That we worship one God in Trinity and Trinity in Unity; Neither confounding the Persons nor dividing the Substance. For there is one Person of the Father: another of the Son: and another of the Holy Ghost. But the Godhead of the Father, of the Son, and of the Holy Ghost, is all one ... For like as we are compelled by the Christian verity: to acknowledge every Person by himself to be God and Lord: so we are forbidden by the Catholic Religion to say, there are three Gods or three Lords ...
>
> Furthermore it is necessary to everlasting salvation: that he also believe rightly the incarnation of our Lord Jesus Christ. For the right Faith is, that we believe and confess: that our Lord Jesus Christ, the Son of God, is God and Man. God, of the Substance of the Father; begotten before all worlds: and Man, of the Substance of his mother, born in the world ... One; not by conversion of the Godhead into flesh: but by the assumption of the Manhood into God. One altogether; not by confusion of substance: but by unity of Person. For as the reasonable soul and flesh is one man: so God and Man is one Christ; Who suffered for our salvation: descended into hell: rose again the third day from the dead. He ascended into heaven, he sitteth on the right hand of God the Father Almighty ... This is the Catholic Faith: which except a man believe truly and firmly, he cannot be saved.[1]

If we were to ask ordinary believers in the pew to explain what exactly this confession means, they will probably be at a loss. Although contemporary believers would grant that these doctrines are fundamental to the Christian faith, most of them, when pressed, would have to admit that they remain puzzling conundrums. How are we to make sense of the claim that the Father and the Son and the Holy Spirit are three distinct persons each of which is to be 'acknowledged by himself to be God and Lord' and yet that they are not three Gods but one 'undivided substance'? Since for us 'persons' are by definition distinct individual agents, it is difficult to see how three persons can be merged into one undivided substance without ceasing to be distinct persons. It seems that the various attempts to solve this conundrum either do so by maintaining the unity at the expense of the Trinity or the Trinity at the expense of the unity.

And how are we to make sense of the claim that Jesus is both wholly God 'of the substance of the Father' and at the same time wholly man 'of the substance of his mother'? If Jesus is 'wholly God' he must presumably have the attributes of divinity like omnipotence, omniscience, omnipresence and so on. If, however, he is 'wholly

---

[1] From the Athanasian Creed. See Philip Schaff, *Creeds of Christendom*, vol. 2 (Grand Rapids, MI, 1977), 66–70.

man' he must be subject to the limitations of human existence, which seem to exclude these divine attributes. It would seem that we could only avoid looking on Jesus as some sort of divine–human schizophrenic by either maintaining his human nature at the expense of his divinity or his divine nature at the expense of his humanity.

Although believers would admit that Jesus 'suffered for our salvation' the way in which this is usually explained seems highly problematical. Of course, by our sinful disobedience to the will of God we fail to honour him in the way that is his due, and thus become estranged from him. However, many believers have great difficulty in accepting that they can only be reconciled with God if God's slighted honour is restored by somebody suffering. It seems as though God wants to see blood before he can accept us again and it does not matter to him whether it is the blood of the guilty ones or the blood of his own innocent Son. Although this is not a logical conundrum like the doctrines of the Trinity and the dual nature of Christ, it is for many a moral one. It seems as though an attitude, which we would consider morally reprehensible in human beings, is quite in order for God. This caused von Harnack to remark that God has the terrible privilege of not being able to forgive out of love but instead always to require payment.[2]

If such doctrines at the heart of the Christian faith involve logical and moral conundrums, is it not asking rather much of us if our salvation is made to depend on our 'truly and firmly' believing them? How can we be required to believe doctrines, which we cannot understand? Can our eternal salvation be made to depend on such a *sacrificium intellectus*? In response it is often said that these doctrines express *mysteries*, which by definition we cannot understand. The nature and ways of God are beyond our finite powers of comprehension. Only in the next life will we be able to gain a clear understanding of what they mean.

> Three in One and One in Three,
> Dimly here we worship thee;
> With the Saints hereafter we
> Hope to bear the palm.

This response tries to justify the *sacrificium intellectus* rather than removing it, and it does so by confusing the puzzles of doctrine with mysteries of faith. Of course, the nature and the ways of God are mysteries for us, but not in the sense that we can know nothing about them or that they are unintelligible to us. On the contrary, we know God and his ways because he reveals himself to us, and to that extent his nature and ways are also intelligible to us. 'Unintelligible knowledge' is a contradiction in terms. On the other hand, God does remain mysterious to us because of the finitude of our existence and the limitations of our knowledge. We only know God to the extent that he reveals himself to us and he only reveals himself to us to the extent that we need to know him in order to live in his fellowship. Our knowledge and understanding of God

---

[2] Adolf von Harnack, *Lehrbuch der Dogmengeschichte*, vol. III (Freiburg iB, 1890), 358.

are therefore adequate but also limited. Beyond these limits they remain a mystery in relation to which we should be agnostic and apophatic. Clearly the divine mysteries require us to be modest in our claims about them and willing to admit the limits of our knowledge and understanding of God. This does not mean, however, that a *sacrificium intellectus* is required of us *within* these limits. One thing of which we can be sure is that God never contradicts himself. What he does reveal to us can therefore never be riddled with logical or moral contradictions. Whenever such contradictions should arise in our understanding of God and his ways, we can be sure that we are mistaken and that we are called upon to revise our understanding in order to remove the contradictions. Our knowledge and understanding of God are not only limited, but also fallible. The puzzles of doctrine are not in God but in our fallible understanding.

In a similar way, all this also applies to our knowledge and understanding of the finite universe. The universe is also mysterious in the sense that there is always more to it than meets the eye. Our knowledge and understanding of finite things are also finite as well as fallible within these limits. When this fallibility gives rise to logical and moral puzzles this is a clear sign that we are mistaken in our claims and that these need revision in order to eliminate the puzzles. Such puzzles are there to be solved and are not to be accepted in a *sacrificium intellectus*.

It is here that Austin Farrer's distinction between mysteries and puzzles is useful.[3] For Farrer, reality (including the reality of God) is mysterious in the sense that there is more to it than we can grasp with our finite capacities for understanding. Such mysteries should be clearly distinguished from the puzzles of doctrine, which arise because of the limitations of the conceptual apparatus in terms of which we understand and describe them. Unlike the mysteries, such puzzles are not located in reality but in our fallible ways of understanding reality. 'Mysteries are not to be solved but (always inadequately) described.'[4] Puzzles, on the other hand, can be solved in principle by revising the conceptual apparatus in terms of which we try to describe the mysteries.

How do we set about describing the nature of things, including the nature of God and his ways with the world? According to Farrer 'our ordinary form of speech informs us how we can do it: we do not ordinarily ask "What is its nature?" but "What is it like?" To describe a thing is to compare it to other things.'[5] This suggests that the conceptual apparatus we employ in describing and understanding God and his ways consists of metaphors, which describe things in terms of their analogies with other things. It is this metaphorical apparatus which gives rise to puzzles:

> God's existence is one of the mysteries of metaphysics, not one of the puzzles of metaphysics … Such mysteries the metaphysician [and the theologian] wrestles with; he attempts to describe them by means of analogies. In his attempt to describe, puzzles certainly arise – puzzles interior to the particular analogical

---

[3] Austin Farrer, *The Glass of Vision* (Glasgow, 1948), 79f.

[4] Farrer, *The Glass of Vision*, 63.

[5] Farrer, *The Glass of Vision*, 75.

description he chooses to employ. Since no analogy fits perfectly, the adaptation of any analogical description to the object described must create puzzles. How is the description to be made either consistent or suitable?[6]

Let us now examine the nature and limits of such analogical or metaphorical use of language. How does such language give rise to puzzles? How can these puzzles be solved by revising or adapting the metaphorical language?

The Limits of Metaphorical Thinking

The term 'metaphor' is ambiguous. For our purposes we can distinguish two senses in which it is used in the theoretical literature on metaphor. On the one hand, it is used, especially in literary theory, to refer to a specific figure of speech, which is distinguished from the literal use of language. On the other hand, the term is also used to refer to a pervasive feature of all human thought and experience. Here the distinction between metaphorical and literal does not apply. We could say that all human thought and experience is metaphorical in this sense.[7]

Sallie McFague describes metaphorical thinking as

> seeing one thing *as* something else, pretending 'this' is 'that' because we do not know how to think or talk about 'this', so we use 'that' as a way of saying something about it. Thinking metaphorically means spotting a thread of similarity between two dissimilar objects, events, or whatever, one of which is better known than the other, and using the better known one as a way of speaking about the lesser known.'[8]

In this sense the term 'metaphor' is used to refer to the conceptual activity in which we understand things by comparing them to each other.

This is an essential feature of all human thought and experience, including human thought and experience of God. One of the most basic conceptual activities characteristic of human thinking is the classification of entities according to the characteristics they have in common.[9] If we wish to gain a hold on the chaos of our sensory impressions, we must recognize the similarities and differences between the things we perceive, and classify them according to these similarities and differences. In perceiving the world we do not merely register chaotic sensory impressions, nor

---

[6] Farrer, *The Glass of Vision*, 79–80.

[7] Elsewhere I have dealt with metaphorical thinking in this sense more extensively than is possible here. See chapter 1 of my *The Model of Love* (Cambridge, 1993). On the relation between metaphorical thinking and the use of metaphor as a figure of speech, see my paper on 'Metaphor and the reality of God', in T.W. Bartel (ed.), *Comparative Theology: Essays for Keith Ward* (London, 2003).

[8] S. McFague, *Metaphorical Theology* (London, 1983), 15.

[9] D.E. Cooper points out the metaphorical nature of classification in *Metaphor* (Oxford, 1966), 139. See also the examples in G. Lakoff and M. Johnson, *Metaphors We Live By* (Chicago, 1980), and my *Theology and Philosophical Inquiry* (London, 1981), 57–63.

do we perceive random undefined objects. We always perceive objects *as belonging to a kind* (people, chairs, tables, houses, trees and so on) and therefore having recognizable characteristics in common and differing in recognizable ways from other objects. This classificatory organization of experience constitutes our horizon for understanding the world: we intuitively seek to understand things by comparing them to similar things with which we are already familiar. I try to understand how *A* works or what value I should attach to *A* by comparing it to *B*, whose working or value I already understand. Understanding the world around us would be impossible without such metaphorical comparison. We understand the nature of something when we see *what it is like*.

Although such metaphorical thinking is indispensable, it also has its limits and can become dangerously misleading when these are ignored. This can happen in two ways. First, comparisons are odious, we say, because they tend to ignore individuality and to treat things that are analogous as though they were identical. After all, everything is itself and not another thing. Hence McFague warns us (in terms derived from Paul Ricoeur) that our generalizing metaphorical concepts 'always contain the whisper, "it is *and it is not*"'.[10] The danger of metaphorical thinking is that we can become so used to the generalizing 'is' that it becomes part of our intuitive pattern of thinking or mental set and we become deaf to the whispered 'and it is not'. It is therefore important to remember that the meanings of the generalizing concepts we employ in our metaphorical thinking are open-ended in the sense that they contain a penumbra of associations, suggestions and implications. When in our metaphorical comparisons we use the same concept in two different contexts or with reference to two different entities, it does not necessarily follow that the whole penumbra of meaning is transferred from the one context to the other. We therefore need critical reflection in order to determine what part of the penumbra of meaning is transferred in each case. Thus, in thinking and speaking of (our relations with) God, we use the same concepts we also use in our thinking and speaking about (our relations with) each other even though we know very well that God is not like other people. Central to theological reflection on the way believers think and speak about God is the task of sorting out critically what part of the penumbra of meaning can and what part cannot be transferred to our thinking and speaking about God. Such reflection does not eliminate the metaphorical nature of our thinking about God, but tries to illuminate its meaning by determining the limits between 'it is' and 'it is not'. All our thinking about God remains metaphorical in the sense that we think and speak about (our relations with) God in terms derived from our thinking and speaking about (our relations with) each other.

Secondly, metaphorical thinking can also become misleading because of its selectivity. This is especially the case when we develop our metaphorical comparisons into conceptual models, that is, 'sustained and systematic metaphors'.[11]

---

[10] McFague, *Metaphorical Theology*, 13.
[11] Max Black, *Models and Metaphors* (Ithaca, NY, 1962), 236.

We do not merely look on *A* as *B* but we try to explore in a sustained and systematic way how far the analogy goes. In this way we try to explore and explain the nature and workings of *A* by comparing it systematically to *B*. Thus in science the behaviour of gases can be fruitfully explained by comparing it systematically with the behaviour of billiard balls, and the behaviour of light rays can be fruitfully explained by comparing it systematically with the behaviour of waves or of moving particles.[12] Although such conceptual models can help us to formulate illuminating questions, they also act as filters, which prevent us from asking other questions. Max Black explains this point with the following example:

> Suppose I am set the task of describing a battle in words drawn as largely as possible from the vocabulary of chess. These latter terms determine a system of implications, which will proceed to control my description of the battle. The enforced choice of the chess vocabulary will lead some aspects of the battle to be emphasized, others to be neglected, and all to be organized in a way that would cause much more strain in other modes of description. The chess vocabulary filters and transforms: it not only selects, it brings forward aspects of the battle that might not be seen at all through another medium.[13]

The conceptual model enables us to discover features of the world, which we would otherwise have overlooked. However, it also filters out other aspects and prevents us from seeing them. No blood can flow in a battle that is looked upon merely as a game of chess. For this reason it is essential that we should guard against making our models absolute and considering the way they enable us to look at the world as the one and only way in which the world should be looked at. Often we need complementary models, which allow us to see things, which we would be prevented from seeing if we used only one model. Thus in the theory of light we need both the wave model and the particle model because each of these enable us to say things about light which the other model would filter out. Sallie McFague summarizes this point neatly as follows:

> Models are necessary ... for they give us something to think about when we do not know what to think, a way of talking when we do not know how to talk. But they are also dangerous, for they exclude other ways of thinking and talking, and in so doing they can easily become literalised, that is, identified as *the* one and only way of understanding a subject. This danger is more prevalent with models than with metaphors because models have a wider range and are more permanent; they also tend to object to competition in ways that metaphors do not.[14]

As in the case of scientific inquiry, some metaphors in religion are also developed in a sustained and systematic way as conceptual models. Thus, in the Christian tradition

---

[12] See Ian Barbour, *Myths, Models and Paradigms* (London, 1974), 30 (on the billiard ball model) and 71f (on the wave and particle models in light theory).

[13] Black, *Models and Metaphors*, 41–2.

[14] McFague, *Metaphorical Theology*, 24.

God is sometimes called a rock (or a 'rock of ages') in order to express his eternal dependability and trustworthiness. Since the analogy between God and a rock does not go much further than that, the rock metaphor does not lend itself for systematic development as a conceptual model. In contrast, God is also talked of as a person, addressed as a person, and so on. The analogy between God and human persons is so rich that it has been developed as the most fundamental and characteristic conceptual model in theistic God-talk. Nevertheless, like all conceptual models, those in theology remain metaphors and, therefore, what they assert is always accompanied by the whisper 'and it is not'. The fruitfulness of personal models for talking about God should, therefore, never make us deaf to the whisper that God is not like other people![15]

Clearly, all the metaphors we employ in talking about God, including those which are systematically developed into conceptual models, remain selective and one-sided. They all need to be complemented or supported by other metaphors in order to bring to light those aspects of the nature and the ways of God, which they filter out or fail to emphasize sufficiently. For this reason the Christian tradition provides a large variety of metaphors in terms of which we can talk and think about God, some of which can be developed into conceptual models in varying degrees of comprehensiveness. This multiplicity of metaphors is well illustrated by the following well-known hymn verse:[16]

> Jesus! my Shepherd, Husband, Friend,
> My Prophet, Priest and King,
> My Lord, my Life, my Way, my End,
> Accept the praise I bring.

These various metaphors complement each other only if we eliminate their implications that contradict each other. Some of them might be developed as conceptual models, while others do not lend themselves for such development and are obviously more suitable in a supporting or complementary role.

Before proceeding further, let us note two other important features of the metaphors in terms of which we think and talk about God. First, our beliefs about the nature and ways of God are *existential* in the sense that they are always directly connected with the ways in which we relate to God. For this reason all the metaphors and models employed in God-talk are primarily relational: they are intended to express the ways in which we ought to relate to God in our actions and attitudes. If we call God a rock, this is meant primarily to indicate the way in which we can depend upon God and only in a secondary, implied, sense to make the factual statement about God that he is the kind of Being on whom we can depend in this way. The ways in

---

[15] Keith Ward gives voice to this whisper in his paper 'Is God a person?', in Gijsbert van den Brink, Luco J. van den Brom and Marcel Sarot (eds), *Christian Faith and Philosophical Theology* (Kampen, 1992), 256–66.

[16] From the hymn 'How sweet the name of Jesus sounds' by John Newton (1725–1807).

which believers relate to God are varied and complex, and in fact comprise their whole way of life in relation to God. For this reason, as we pointed out above, we require a large variety of complementary and mutually supportive metaphors in order to express all the various aspects of this relation. All such religious metaphors are primarily commissive or 'self-involving', to use the term coined by Donald Evans.[17] Thus, in the hymn quoted above, all the metaphors used to refer to Jesus express commitments to various ways of relating to Jesus in our actions and attitudes. More in general, all our talk about God is at the same time talk about ourselves in the sense that it expresses our commitment to a comprehensive form of life in relation to God.

Secondly, the claim that all talk of God is commissive, does not entail a non-cognitive or non-realist view of religious belief. In fact, the actions and attitudes to which believers commit themselves when understanding their lives in terms of their beliefs become incoherent if they were to reject the factual claims involved in the beliefs. It would be incoherent to live my life as a life in the presence of God if I were to deny that there really is a God in whose presence I live! Since the truth of the belief is a constitutive presupposition of the form of life, the latter would be incoherent if the former is denied.[18] R.W. Hepburn provides a good illustration of this point:

> If I say, 'the Lord is my strength and shield', and if I am a believer, I may experience feelings of exultation and be confirmed in an attitude of quiet confidence. If, however, I tell myself that the arousal of such feelings and confirming of attitude is *the* function of the sentence, that despite appearances it does not refer to a state of affairs, then the more I reflect on this the less I shall exult and the less appropriate my attitude will seem. For there was no magic in the sentence by virtue of which it mediated feelings and confirmed attitudes: these were *responses* to the kind of Being to whom, I trusted, the sentence referred: and response is possible only so long as that exists to which or to whom the response is made.[19]

Truth claims cannot be eliminated from religion. Religious metaphors are therefore 'reality depicting'[20] and religious faith entails some form of critical realism.[21] Yet, such religious claims differ from those in science by being necessarily related to the religious form of life: religious truth claims are made with reference to the factual presuppositions, which are constitutive for the form of life. For this reason they are 'existential' in a way that the truth claims of science are not. It might make sense to say: 'It is true that the planet Jupiter exists and is the largest planet of our solar system, but I don't really care much about that.' It is, however, absurd to say: 'It is true

---

[17] See Donald Evans, *The Logic of Self-Involvement* (London, 1963).

[18] On the role of such constitutive presuppositions, see my papers on 'Wittgenstein and the irrationality of rational theology', in J.M. Byrne, *The Christian Understanding of God* (Dublin, 1993) and 'Wittgenstein and the Anselmian project', *Bijdragen*, 60, (1999).

[19] R.W. Hepburn, 'Poetry and religious belief', in A. MacIntyre (ed.), *Metaphysical Beliefs* (London, 1957), 148.

[20] Janet Soskice, *Metaphor and Religious Language* (Oxford, 1985), ch. 7.

[21] On critical realism, see Ian Barbour, *Myths, Models and Paradigms*, ch. 3.

that God exists and is the personal creator of the universe, but I don't really care much about that.' Religious truth claims become meaningless when they are divorced in this way from the context of the religious form of life of which they are the constitutive presuppositions.

The Puzzles of Metaphorical Thinking

We have now explained how believers try to understand the nature and the ways of God in terms of metaphor. They try to understand what God and his ways *are like*. Such metaphorical thinking is subject to various limits and conceptual puzzles arise in our understanding of God when we fail to recognize these limits. This can happen in various ways. First, we can fail in our metaphorical comparisons to recognize the differences between the entities, which we compare with each other. We treat entities that are analogical as though they were identical and become deaf to the whisper that they are different. When in this way we become deaf to the whisper that God is not like other people, we end up with an unacceptable form of anthropomorphism in our understanding of God and his ways.

Secondly, we can overlook the one-sidedness and selectivity of our metaphors and conceptual models, and refuse to complement or support them with other metaphors. The result is a one-sided view of God, which often amounts to heresy. A good example of this is Arius of whom Bethune-Baker writes as follows:

> Arius seems, in part at least, to have been misled by a wrong use of analogy, and by mistaking description for definition. All attempts to explain the nature and relations of the Deity must largely depend on metaphor, and no one metaphor can exhaust those relations. Each metaphor can only describe one aspect of the nature or being of the Deity, and the inferences which can be drawn from it have their limits when they conflict with the inferences which can be truly drawn from other metaphors describing other aspects. From one point of view Sonship is a true description of the inner relations of the Godhead: from another point of view the title Logos describes them best. Each metaphor must be limited by the other. The title Son may obviously imply later origin and a distinction amounting to ditheism. It is balanced by the other title Logos, which implies co-eternity and inseparable union. Neither title exhausts the relations. Neither may be pressed so far as to exclude the other.[22]

Thirdly, even when we do employ complementary and supporting metaphors, this can result in logical puzzles when the implications of these various metaphors conflict with each other. In the words of Bethune-Baker, 'each metaphor can only describe one aspect of the nature or being of the Deity, and the inferences which can be drawn from it have their limits when they conflict with the inferences which can be

---

[22] J.F. Bethune-Baker, *An Introduction to the Early History of Christian Doctrine* (London, 1958), 160. Recent scholarship casts some doubt on Bethune-Baker's interpretation of Arius. However, this does not affect the point illustrated by the example.

truly drawn from other metaphors describing other aspects'. Thus the metaphor of Christ as the Son of God can seem to contradict the metaphor of Christ as the Son of man. In such a case we should seek ways of developing these metaphors that do not contradict each other. In Chapter 5 I explore ways of eliminating this fundamental puzzle in Christology.

Fourthly, changes in our cultural framework of understanding or in the demands of life with which we are faced, could make certain metaphors incomprehensible in our current ways of thought, or irrelevant and inadequate for making sense of the contemporary demands of life. This could make such metaphors unsuitable for expressing the nature of God to us today. As I show in Chapters 4, 5 and 6, the Platonist framework of thought that came naturally to the Church Fathers is now so strange to us that the metaphors derived from it have become quite unsuitable for explaining Christian doctrine to us today. Similarly, we have become so unfamiliar with the feudal concept of 'honour' and the legal framework in terms of which the doctrine of atonement was developed in the twelfth century, that this doctrine now seems to present us with a moral conundrum. In such cases we should rather employ other metaphors from the biblical tradition or at least radically reinterpret these metaphors in ways that make them intelligible to us today. In Chapters 3 and 4 I explore ways of eliminating this moral conundrum from the doctrine of atonement.

Fifthly, the models and metaphors in terms of which we try to understand the nature of God and his ways are often developed in purely theoretical terms. The question is then merely one of gaining a theoretical understanding of the nature of God quite apart from the existential nature of our relationship with God. In this way doctrines become speculative exercises regarding the nature of God in himself rather than ways of understanding the meaning and significance of our lives in relation to God and the assumptions about the nature of God and his ways which underlie such understanding. For many believers such doctrines become irrelevant intellectual exercises that do not concern them personally. Doctrines seem to be relevant only to academic theologians who have a merely intellectual interest in such issues. It then becomes essential to reinterpret such doctrines in order to show how they help us to understand the meaning and significance of our lives. The metaphors and conceptual models in terms of which such doctrines are formulated should be developed in ways that emphasize their existential significance. In Chapters 2 and 3 I discuss the context of human life within which I suggest the fundamental doctrines of the Christian faith should be interpreted in order to bring out their existential meaning.

Theology and the Puzzles of Doctrine

It belongs to the task of systematic theology to seek ways of eliminating such puzzles from our understanding of God and his ways. To do so theologians have to explore which inferences may be validly drawn from the conceptual models of a religious tradition and how this can be done without giving rise to conceptual puzzles.

Wittgenstein makes some useful points in this connection. For Wittgenstein, religious belief can be viewed as a specific form of life in which religious believers participate. It is the form of life in which believers try to make sense of their lives and their experience of the world around them by relating life and the world to God in terms of the metaphors and conceptual models derived from their religious tradition. My life is meaningful because God loves me and I am a child of God. The world around me is meaningful because God has created it his wonders to proclaim, and so on, and so on. In order to partake in this form of life, we need to be introduced into the language-game expressing it and into the use of the metaphors and models that characterize it. In this connection Wittgenstein says that we have to learn 'the technique of using a picture'.[23] It is part of the task of theology to explain this technique to us by making explicit the implicit 'conceptual grammar' of the religious language-game. Doing this involves determining the 'logical limits' of the language-game and of the use of the pictures employed in it.

The 'logical limits' to the use of a religious picture have to do with the inferences that can or cannot be validly drawn from it within the religious language-game. I master the technique of using the picture when I know which inferences I can and which I cannot draw from it. Wittgenstein illustrates this point in the light of the picture: 'God's eye sees everything.' Which inferences could a believer draw from this picture, and which inferences would be invalid within the religious language-game? Obviously, a believer would say that, since God's eye sees everything, God is aware of all that happens, not only in the world but also in the hearts and minds of all people: 'Almighty God, unto whom all hearts be open, all desires known, and from whom no secrets are hidden ...' However, Wittgenstein asks the rhetorical question: 'Are eyebrows going to be talked of, in connection with the Eye of God?'[24] Here we have clearly reached the 'logical limits' of the picture. It is conceivable that a child might ask after the eyebrows of God. It is, however, part of the child's introduction to the religious language-game to learn that such a question is out of order since it transgresses the 'logical limits' of the language-game. For this reason the catechism not only teaches us to give the right answers but also to ask the right questions!

There is a second kind of inference we must also learn to draw if we are to master the technique. Since the religious language-game is embedded in the religious form of life, using the religious picture entails that we commit ourselves to this form of life. Saying 'almighty God, unto whom all hearts be open, all desires known, and from whom no secrets are hidden ...', commits the speaker to a complex set of feelings, attitudes and actions which follows from looking on life in the world in terms of this picture. Uttering these words would become absurd if we were to deny the entailed commitment. Such commissive implications are also an essential part of the conceptual grammar of the religious language-game. Understanding the language-

---

[23] Ludwig Wittgenstein, *Lectures and Conversations on Aesthetics, Psychology and Religious Belief* (Oxford, 1966), 63, 71–2.

[24] Wittgenstein, *Lectures and Conversations*, 71.

game is only possible if we know how to participate in the form of life in which it is embedded. This requires that we learn which commissive implications can be drawn from the metaphors and conceptual models we use to think and talk about God and his ways. Here, too, we must learn to know the limits of our metaphors. Not only is God not like other people, but our actions and attitudes in relation to God are also not like those in relation to other people, even though we try to understand the former by comparing them to the latter. In calling Jesus 'my Prophet, Priest and King', I do relate to Jesus as to a prophet, a priest and a king. However, this does not deny the fact that in many ways the attitudes and actions appropriate in relation to Jesus will also be very different from those we would adopt towards an Isaiah, an Aaron or a David. Here too the analogy is limited and we cannot transfer the whole penumbra of meaning of the metaphors.

I have argued that it belongs to the task of theology to sort out critically which part of the penumbra of meaning of our religious metaphors can be transferred to our thinking and speaking about (our relations with) God. Are there any criteria in the light of which this can be done? Is what Wittgenstein calls 'the technique of using the picture' something which we can only master intuitively or are there rules by which it can be regulated? How are we to determine the logical limits of our metaphors?

One possible answer is that we should test our understanding of the metaphors in the light of divine revelation. In the words of Austin Farrer, 'we suppose in general that the applicability of images is to be tested by looking away from the images to the things they symbolize'. This will not do, however, since

> in the case of supernatural divine revelation, nothing but the images is given us to act as an indication of the reality. We cannot appeal from the images to the reality, for by hypothesis we have not got the reality, except in the form of that which the images signify.[25]

In other words, 'the theologian cannot simply feel the adequacy or inadequacy of the revealed images to the object they describe: for he has not that object. He cannot criticize the revealed images from his acquaintance with their object: he can only confront them with one another.'[26] We cannot do more than confront the various metaphors with each other and see to it that the inferences we draw from the one do not conflict with those drawn from the other. This brings us back to Bethune-Baker's suggestion that 'inferences which can be drawn from [one metaphor] have their limits when they conflict with the inferences which can be truly drawn from other metaphors describing other aspects … Neither may be pressed so far as to exclude the other.'[27] Although this suggestion is helpful, it is not sufficient to eliminate our problem completely. When the inferences which can be drawn from two metaphors conflict, we can interpret them consistently by making one the primary metaphor

---

[25] Farrer, *The Glass of Vision*, 58.

[26] Farrer, *The Glass of Vision*, 76.

[27] Bethune-Baker, *An Introduction to the Early History of Christian Doctrine*, 160.

which we develop as a conceptual model and giving the other a secondary role as supportive or complementary to the primary metaphor. In this way the inferences drawn from the one are given preference above those drawn from the other even though neither metaphor is 'pressed so far as to exclude the other'. But then we still have to decide which metaphors are to be developed as conceptual models and which metaphors are taken to be merely supportive or complementary. Thus we call God loving, just, holy, wise, powerful, and so on. Which of these metaphors is central to our understanding of God and which is subordinate? Which are we to develop as key models and which are we to interpret as supportive or complementary? Different decisions on this point can result in widely differing ideas on the nature of God. The question remains, therefore, how are we to make such decisions?

A different approach is taken in the medieval theories of analogy. One of the most important forms of analogy discussed here is the analogy of proportionality. According to this form of analogy, when the same property is ascribed to both God and human beings, it is ascribed to each in proportion to his own nature. Thus God is wise in proportion to the divine nature and human beings are wise in proportion to human nature. This would be helpful if we were to have direct non-metaphorical access to the nature of God. However, as Farrer points out, we do not know the nature of God apart from the metaphors that express it.

A possible response to this difficulty is to claim that there are some second-order characteristics given in the definition of the divine that qualify all divine attributes and thus distinguish them from human attributes. Thus, in accordance with Anselm's definition of God as 'that than which nothing greater can be conceived', so-called perfect-being theology argues that all perfections or 'great-making properties' which can be ascribed to human beings also have to be ascribed to God, albeit to an infinite degree. While humans can be wise, powerful, loving, knowing and so on, God is infinitely wise, powerful, loving, knowing and so on. In the words of Paul Helm,

> perfect being theology thus invites us to think of God … as a Herculean figure, able, as it were, to out-lift and out-throw and out-run all his opponents, and to perform such activities maximally … Whatever the most powerful of his creatures can do, God can do it to an infinitely greater degree.[28]

In this way the great-making qualities of human beings have to be maximized in order to apply to God.

This kind of perfect-being theology is flawed in two important respects. First, it reduces the difference between God and human persons to one of degree, and therefore fails to account for the qualitative difference between the divine and the human. God becomes merely Superman. Secondly, divine perfection is the standard or ideal by which our contingent and fallible ideas of what counts as perfection have

---

[28] P. Helm, *The Perfect and the Particular* (London, 1994), 18.

to be judged and, therefore, cannot simply be the maximizing of these ideas. Roger White points out that this approach fails to recognize 'the extent to which natural man may have either no idea, or a perverse misconception of what the ideal alluded to by the word may be like'.[29] Karl Barth is therefore right in saying that we have no a priori knowledge of divine perfection. Christians claim that we can only come to know it a posteriori in light of the way God reveals himself to us in his dealing with the people of Israel and in the life and teaching of Jesus Christ. This revelation often contradicts the ideals of perfection maintained by natural man: 'What the believer calls "success" will be failure in the eyes of the world, what he calls "joy" will seem like grief, what he calls "victory" will seem like certain defeat. So it was, Christians believe, at the Cross of Christ.'[30] From this it is clear that we can only transfer the penumbra of meaning of our human concepts to our talk of God to the extent that it is consistent with the way in which God reveals himself to us, as Christians believe, in Christ and in the Bible.

In spite of these objections, perfect-being theology can also be interpreted in a more qualitative and less quantitative way, and thus provide us with a useful rule of thumb complementing the appeal to revelation. God is perfect, not in the sense that his perfections are the maximization of ours, but in the sense that he is free from the limitations of human finitude. Thus our knowledge is always limited, whereas God knows everything that it is logically possible to know. Our capacities are limited and we cannot do just anything, whereas God can do anything that is logically possible to do and that is consistent with the divine character as revealed to us.[31] Our weakness of will (*akrasia*) limits our ability to do what is good, whereas God is free from *akrasia* and, therefore, perfectly good in the sense that everything he does is good.[32] As spatio-temporal beings our capacities are limited by our finite spatio-temporal location, whereas God is eternal and omnipresent and therefore free from such spatio-temporal limitations. This difference between the divine and the human has far-reaching implications for all the characteristics that we can ascribe to God and, thus, for the extent in which the penumbra of meaning of our human concepts can be transferred to our talk of God.[33]

We have said that this is a useful rule of thumb complementing the appeal to revelation. However, this does not eliminate the problem that revelation as such is given to us in terms of a wide variety of metaphors that have to be interpreted

[29] R. White, 'Notes on analogical predication and speaking about God', in B. Hebblethwaite and S.R. Sutherland (eds), *The Philosophical Frontiers of Christian Theology* (Cambridge, 1982), 223.

[30] D.Z. Phillips, *Faith and Philosophical Enquiry* (London, 1970), 83. See also Paul Helm's detailed analysis of this point in *The Perfect and the Particular*, and White, 'Notes on analogical predication'.

[31] On divine omniscience and omnipotence, see chapter 3 of my *What Are We Doing When We Pray?* (London, 1984).

[32] On this point see my *What Are We Doing When We Pray?*, 33, 40, and chapter 4 of my *Speaking of a Personal God* (Cambridge, 1992).

[33] In chapters 7–9 of *The Model of Love* I give a detailed analysis of the penumbra of meaning of the human concept of love and show how God's freedom from the limitations of human finitude determines the extent to which this penumbra of meaning can be transferred to our talk of the love of God.

consistently with each other. We therefore still have to decide which metaphors are to be developed as conceptual models and which are supportive or complementary. How we do this will determine our overall view of God. As we have argued, each such model of God remains a metaphor, albeit a developed one, and as such it remains one-sided. Each will present another face of God and God has many faces for he is a living God who reveals himself in manifold ways in his dealings with us. Thus believers will claim that God is ever present to us in ways that are relevant and adequate to the demands we have to face in the specific circumstances or times in which we live. For this reason we need to develop a variety of models of God in order to experience the presence of God in ways which are relevant and adequate to the changing circumstances in which we live. If we make one such model of God absolute and claim that it alone presents the true face of God, we will be defending a static view of God that is in danger of becoming irrelevant or inadequate: 'In order to do theology, one must in each epoch do it differently. To refuse this task is to settle for a theology appropriate to some other time than one's own.'[34]

It is clear that pragmatic considerations also determine the way in which we interpret the metaphors by means of which the living God reveals himself to us in the ever-changing circumstances of our lives.[35] This again emphasizes the existential nature of divine revelation. God makes himself known to us to the extent that is necessary in order to enable us to experience his fellowship in the concrete circumstances in which we find ourselves. What we need to say about God is therefore limited to the constitutive presuppositions of our spirituality and our concrete life of fellowship with God. All implications of the metaphors of faith that are not relevant to these presuppositions are therefore to be ignored. Thus when talking about the all-seeing eye of God, the implication that God can see into our hearts and know all our thoughts and desires so that we cannot keep these secret from him is very relevant for our life and spirituality, whereas implications about eyebrows are not. The existential nature of our God-talk therefore excludes mere intellectual speculation about how God is apart from the way we relate to him in our spirituality and in the life of faith. Here again we encounter the logical limits of our God-talk. Beyond this point the reality of God remains mysterious. Here we can only be agnostic and apophatic. Here God 'dwells in unapproachable light' (1 Timothy 6:16). *Within* these limits, however, we cannot afford to be apophatic. Our spirituality and our fellowship with God are *human* and therefore we must be able to spell out the constitutive presuppositions of this spirituality and of this life of fellowship in human terms or else our spirituality and fellowship with God would collapse into an incomprehensible something, we know not what.

It is now clear that there are two ways in which we can confuse the puzzles of doctrine with the mysteries of faith, both of which should be avoided. On the one hand, we could look on the puzzles of doctrine as incomprehensible mysteries that we

---

[34] Salie McFague, *Models of God* (London, 1987), 30.
[35] See my *The Model of Love*, 19–29.

should merely accept and not try to solve. This turns the commitment of faith into a *sacrificium intellectus.* On the other hand, we could treat the mysteries of faith as mere logical puzzles for which we are to seek speculative solutions. Such speculative prying into the 'inner nature of the Godhead' apart from the ways in which God relates to us, is a form of intellectual hubris, which ignores the limits of our knowledge and understanding of God. Within these limits we should do our best to achieve a coherent understanding of the ways in which God relates to us. Beyond these limits it behoves us to remain agnostic and apophatic.

Conclusion

At the beginning of this chapter I argued that central doctrines of the Christian faith, such as the doctrines of the Trinity, the dual nature of Christ and the Atonement seem to confront us with logical or moral conundrums which make these doctrines unintelligible to many ordinary believers. Furthermore, these doctrines strike many ordinary believers as mere theoretical constructions produced by academic theologians. As such they fail to see what existential relevance such doctrines have for their lives. What is needed is a way of interpreting these doctrines that is conceptually coherent, intelligible in terms of our contemporary framework of understanding, and existentially relevant. In the chapters that follow I develop proposals for understanding these doctrines in a way that satisfies these requirements.

In Chapters 2 and 3 I describe the existential context or 'matrix of faith' within which these doctrines should be understood. In Chapter 2 I discuss the nature of human happiness and argue that in the Christian tradition such happiness can ultimately be achieved only in a life of loving fellowship with God. In Chapter 3 I argue that such a happy life in the love of God can only be attained if we become reconciled with the God from whom we have become estranged.

Chapters 4–6 are devoted to a critical analysis of the doctrines of Atonement, Christology and the Trinity as the way in which the matrix of faith has traditionally been interpreted in Christian theology ever since these doctrines were first developed by the Church Fathers. One important reason why we have difficulty making sense of these doctrines today is the fact that the Fathers conceptualized them in terms of the Platonic thought-forms of their time. Since these forms of thought have now become quite strange to us, these doctrines have to be reinterpreted in terms that are more accessible to ordinary believers in our time. In Chapter 4 I discuss of the doctrine of Atonement as an explanation of the way in which reconciliation with God is possible. Chapter 5 explores the role that Jesus has to fulfil in order to make such reconciliation possible, and the kind of being we assume him to be in order to fulfil this role. In what sense is Jesus human and in what sense is he divine? Chapter 6 discusses the doctrine of the Trinity in the light of the way in which the Father, the Son and the Spirit are all three involved in our reconciliation. What does this entail for the relation between the three?

In a brief final chapter I explore the extent to which my proposed reinterpretation of Christian doctrine can contribute to the dialogue between the three Abrahamic traditions of faith: Judaism, Christianity and Islam.

PART 2
FELLOWSHIP WITH GOD:
THE MATRIX OF FAITH

CHAPTER 2

Ultimate Happiness and Fellowship with God

Rich and Famous

Ultimate happiness is something we enjoy when we achieve the good life. But what is the 'good life'? Different religions and views of life propose a variety of ideals of the good life to which their adherents should aspire. Irrespective of whether or not we subscribe to any of these, the ideal to which *in practice* many of us aspire in life can be symbolized by two terms: to be 'rich and famous'. In fact, all religions and views of life usually assume that being 'rich and famous' is in an important sense a necessary condition for ultimate happiness.

First we would like to be rich, but not necessarily in the sense of being wealthy. Wealth is not an end in itself but merely the means to achieve our ends, and as such not even the sufficient means. We also need to have the physical, intellectual and personal capacities as well as the opportunities to become that which each of us would like to be and thus to realize what we consider to be our own true interests in life. This need not necessarily be to live a life of luxury. It could also be to achieve success in business or in academic life or in sport or in some other sphere of human endeavour. In short, each one of us seeks to achieve that individual ideal of a good life, which constitutes his or her chosen self-image, and in achieving which he or she hopes to realize his or her individual identity as a person.

In this connection Plato distinguishes the imperfect way each individual actualizes the Good or the Beautiful from the perfect potentiality which each individual has for realizing the Good or the Beautiful in his or her own person. What Plato lets Alcibiades say of Socrates, could be applied to every person: 'He is exactly like the busts of Selinus, which are set up in the statuaries' shops, holding pipes or flutes in their mouths; and they are made to open in the middle and they have images of gods inside them' (*Symposium* 215A\B). The clay bust represents his observable characteristics or appearance to the world, and is always to some degree flawed and misshapen. Thus Socrates, like the semi-deity Selinus, was known for his lack of elegance and physical beauty. But this is merely his imperfect actuality. Inside the misshapen clay bust there is a golden figurine of a god. This is his ideal potentiality to realize the Good. This hidden potentiality is known as one's *daimon*. It is inborn and constitutes one's true self and one's identity as a person. To know yourself in the Socratic sense is to know your daimon. This daimon subsists in you not as an actuality, a finished product, but as a possibility, as a task to be realized. To know yourself in the Socratic sense means to know the ideal potentiality that it is your task and responsibility to realize progressively in your life. To achieve ultimate happiness consists, therefore, in being able to realize your individual daimon.[1] For this reason we all desire to be 'rich' in the extended sense of knowing our individual daimon and having the means, the abilities and the opportunities to realize it in life.

Furthermore, each person's daimon is unique and constitutes his or her personal identity as an individual. It is a form of perfection different from that of every other person. You alone and no one else in your stead can realize your daimon in the world. You are irreplaceable when it comes to realizing your own individual potentiality for the Good. If society should try to force you to conform to some common ideal of the Good, this would violate your individual identity as a person and prevent you from realizing your daimon in life. According to Jean-Paul Sartre we should therefore choose our individual identity ourselves and not have an identity thrust on us by others. In fact, we have the power to fight against and reject the identity that others try to foist on us. Acquiescing in it is sinking into 'bad faith'.[2] You and you alone should decide what is good for you and what you are to be in your life, and thus authentically choose your own identity.

On the other hand, there is a limit to the range of identities from which you can choose. You cannot just claim any identity you please. As Sartre points out, I cannot choose to be a famous concert pianist or to be the shah of Persia since these are not options open to me. Your freedom to choose your identity is a concrete freedom in the sense that it is limited to the options given to you in the concrete circumstances of life in which you find yourself. Many ideals are excluded for you when you lack the means, the capacities or the opportunities to pursue them in your life. Furthermore, since your existence as a person is not solipsistic, the realization of your daimon affects not only yourself but others as well. To the extent that you fail to know your daimon and to live in truth with it, and therefore become distracted from your destiny, the unique value that you represent will be lacking from the world and everyone will be the poorer. For this reason it is in everybody's interest that you should realize your daimon in the world. In recognizing you to be a person with this unique potentiality for the Good, others do not only help you to be the person you are called to be. They also identify with you by recognizing your good as part of their own and sharing responsibility with you for realizing it. It follows that your identity claim can only be upheld to the extent that others endorse it and recognize you to be the person you aim to be. Your identity as a person is neither determined by yourself alone, nor is it foisted upon you by others, but it is constituted by a consensus in which others endorse your chosen ideal in life. Persons can interact intelligibly only on the basis of such an agreement or consensus about who each of them is to be. Thus Dwight Van de Vate points out that the cliché lunatic who claims to be Napoleon imposes impossible

---

[1] On this connection between personal identity and individual ideals for the good life, see my 'Religious belief and personal identity', *Neue Zeitschrift für systematische Theologie und Religionsphilosophie*, 38 (1996), 155–65.

[2] Jean-Paul Sartre, *Being and Nothingness* (New York, 1956), ch. 2.

identity requirements on those who would interact with him as if he were sane. Hence they declare him to be mad.[3] Similarly, the delinquent who chooses to pursue a life of crime fails to receive the endorsement of others and is locked up and excluded from society. To be ultimately happy, it is therefore not sufficient that we are able to decide authentically what ideal in life is to constitute our personal identity, nor that we merely acquire the means, the capacities and the opportunities to pursue this ideal in life. We also need our personal ideals to be endorsed and our chosen identity to be recognized and appreciated by others. In order to be ultimately happy, therefore, we need not only to be 'rich' but also to be 'famous'.

A classic example of someone who strove to become 'rich and famous' in the above sense, was the prodigal son in the parable of Jesus. According to Luke 15, the son went to his father and demanded his share of the inheritance. Having received this, he decided to free himself from the dictates of his father and use his inheritance to realize his own self-chosen ideals in life. He wanted to 'do his own thing' and live a life of luxury without want, of pleasure without pain and also to enjoy the adulation of his friends (referred to later by his brother as 'his women' (v. 30)). Unfortunately his endeavours went badly wrong. In the words of Luke,

> he turned the whole of his share into cash and left home for a distant country where he squandered it in dissolute living. He had spent it all, when a severe famine fell upon that country and he began to be in need. So he went and attached himself to one of the local landowners, who sent him onto his farm to mind the pigs. He would have been glad to fill his belly with the pods that the pigs were eating, but no one gave him anything. (Luke 15:14–16).

Of course, his downfall was largely his own fault. His chosen ideal of a good life was clearly questionable. He failed miserably to achieve Socratic self-knowledge and to know his true daimon. His fundamental mistake was furthermore that he ignored the *finitude* of his human existence. He squandered his inheritance as though there were no end to it. But unfortunately his means were finite. And then, to compound his misfortune, the famine came which he could not have foreseen or have done anything to prevent. Both his knowledge and his capacities were finite. To cap it all, his friends turned out to be fair-weather friends. The endorsement and recognition he received from them turned out to be finite too. The value bestowed on him as a person by the recognition of his friends seemed to evaporate. In the end he felt himself to be worthless in the eyes of everybody. Nobody cared about him, or would even grant him to fill his belly with the pods the pigs were eating.

It is clear from this example that within the limits of our finite human existence, the happiness we are able to achieve will be no more than finite. First, our Socratic self-knowledge necessarily remains finite and fallible. More often than not we are mistaken about the nature of our daimon. Secondly, even if we were to know our true daimon, our ability to realize it remains finite too. It remains an ideal that more often

---

[3] Dwight Van de Vate, *Romantic Love* (London, 1981), 23.

than not we fail to achieve. We remain unable to finally realize it since our lives, our means, our knowledge and our capacities remain finite and there is a limit to the extent to which we can count on each other for endorsement and acknowledgement. Our 'riches and fame' remain limited. We are not infinite, omniscient, omnipotent and ever dependable like God. Thirdly, even if we were to know our true daimon and have the ability to achieve it in our lives, this does not necessarily make us happy since there is also a limit to our will for the Good. Knowing what is good for us does not mean that we also desire to do it. In fact, as humans we often tend to desire those things that we know are not good for us. When we do what is good, we therefore do so out of a sense of duty rather than from desire. We do the good because we have to rather than because we want to. But in that case realizing the good in our lives cannot really make us happy. Clearly, *ultimate* happiness, the final realization of our true daimon, necessarily remains an ideal to which we may aspire and thereby find direction in our lives, but it can never be finally realised in our human state of finitude. The dilemmas faced by the prodigal son are fundamentally the dilemmas given in our human condition.

Religious traditions and views of life propose a variety of ideals of the good life that could provide direction for our lives and the achievement of which is claimed to make us ultimately happy. Usually they also suggest ways in which we should strive after ultimate happiness and ways in which we might overcome the limitations of human finitude. Thus in the Christian tradition the ideal of ultimate happiness has often been sought in the enjoyment of the loving fellowship of God. A proponent of this ideal is St Augustine. He argues in his *De Moribus Ecclesiae Catholicae*[4] that 'no one can be happy who does not enjoy what is man's chief good, nor is there anyone who enjoys this who is not happy' (*De Moribus* 3.4). But what is this chief good for human existence? It must be something 'than which there is nothing better' and at the same time something 'which cannot be lost against the will. For no one can feel confident regarding a good, which he knows can be taken from him, although he wishes to keep and cherish it. But if a man feels no confidence regarding the good which he enjoys, how can he be happy while in such fear of losing it?' (*De Moribus* 3.5). It is clear, says Augustine, that God is the only Being who can fulfil these requirements: 'Our chief good, which we must hasten to arrive at in preference to all other things, is nothing else than God.' Since nothing can separate us from his love, this must be 'surer as well as better than any other good' (*De Moribus* 11.18). From this Augustine concludes that 'God then alone must be loved; and all this world, that is, all sensible things ... are to be used as this life requires' (*De Moribus* 20.37). Since our human 'riches and fame' are finite and since we know that they can be taken from us although we wish to keep and cherish them, they cannot provide us with ultimate happiness. Instead, Augustine advises, we should seek our ultimate happiness in the

---

[4] Quotations taken from 'On the morals of the Christian Church', in Philip Schaff (ed.), *The Nicene and Post-Nicene Fathers*, vol. IV, (Grand Rapids, MI, 1979). For an extended discussion on Augustine's views on the love of God, see my *The Model of Love*, ch. 5.

love of God since that cannot be taken from us against our will. For Augustine, then, ultimate happiness consists in the enjoyment (*frui*) of the loving fellowship of God.[5]

This Augustinian view on ultimate happiness is also reflected in the way in which Christian mystics like Bernard of Clairvaux understood the *unio mystica*, the mystic union with God that is the goal of the mystic's life. The *via mystica*, the route along which the mystic seeks ultimate happiness, culminates in the enjoyment of a loving union with God. Mysticism is however not a uniform phenomenon and various mystics have held a variety of views on the nature of this mystic union with God[6]. Thus, for example, unitive mystics like Eckhard, Tauler and Suso who were influenced by Denis (the Areopagite) and the Neoplatonism of Plotinus, tended to interpret the *unio mystica* as a kind of 'fusion' in which the personal individuality of the mystic is eliminated. Ultimate happiness then becomes a kind of 'deification' in which the individual existence of the mystic is merged into 'the divine'. As I show in Chapter 4, this view is analogous to patristic ideas on salvation as a form of divination. Another interpretation of the mystic union, which is especially popular in contemporary literature on mysticism influenced by the work of William James, emphasizes the experiential aspects of mysticism. Here the mystic union is taken to be an ecstatic experience and the *via mystica* as a way to achieve such experiences. Bernard, however, understood the mystic union with God as a loving relationship analogous to relationships of love between human persons. In his sermons on the Song of Songs, Bernard explored this analogy in detail. Of course, this can be no more than an analogy since God is not like other people nor is the love of God like human love. In order to understand how mystics like Bernard conceived of ultimate happiness, we need to explore the limits of this analogy between divine and human love.

In the following sections of this chapter I discuss the relevant features of love relationships between human beings (next section), and the most important ways in which the love of God differs from human love and how this love can provide the anchor of our ultimate happiness (third section). Finally, I discuss the way in which human unhappiness results from the fact that we are estranged from God.

Human Love

What is the nature of a relationship of mutual love or fellowship between humans?[7] For our present purposes we could distinguish five aspects, which are characteristic of such relationships.

---

[5] Augustine's eudaimonistic ideal of the good life is perfectly expressed in the answer to the first question in the *Westminster Shorter Catechism* of 1647: 'Man's chief end is to glorify God and enjoy Him forever (*Deum glorificare eodemque frui in aeternum*).'

[6] For an extended analysis of the various views on the nature of mysticism, see my *The Model of Love*, ch. 3.

[7] For an extended analysis of the nature of such relationships, see chapters 7–9 of my *The Model of Love*.

First, in such relationships each partner strives to know and to serve the true interests of the other, and not primarily his or her own interests. Or rather, each partner *identifies* with the other by treating the interests of the other as his or her own interests. By this identification, your interests have become my own and I serve them as being my own. Your daimon is incorporated in my own. By thus serving your interests as my own, I love you as myself. In this sense such relationships are primarily relationships of mutual identification:

> If I love someone I care for him. I want his good, not merely as much as I want my own, but as being my own … Aristotle's definition of a friend as a *heteros autos*, another self, catches exactly the ambiguity … I remain different from you, but we are of one mind in wanting and hoping for those things that are good for you, and in fearing whatever is bad.[8]

It is here that loving fellowship differs from contractual agreements or business relations in which two persons accept certain rights and obligations towards each other. Thus in an agreement between an employer and an employee, the employer assumes the obligation to pay the employee a wage in exchange for the right to the labour which the employee has to provide for the employer, whereas the employee is given the right to receive wages in exchange for the obligation to provide labour for the employer. People enter into such agreements explicitly, or often tacitly, with a view to the advantage that each party can gain for him or herself. I am not concerned with you personally or with furthering your interests but with procuring your services to further my own interests. I earn the right to your services by fulfilling my obligations towards you. Often our relations with other people can best be described as tacit agreements of this kind that do not aim at loving fellowship.

A second characteristic of loving fellowship is that the partners are for each other unique and irreplaceable. Here again love differs from business relations where I serve your interests in order that you might serve mine in return. Since I merely try to buy or earn your services, you have for me a merely *instrumental value* as a means to further my own interests. You are therefore replaceable for me by any other means as effective for this purpose. My relationship is not with you as an irreplaceable individual but as a replaceable means to further my own interests:

> If I do business with you … my good will towards you is conditional and limited. I will keep my side of the bargain provided you keep yours. Your value in my eyes is contingent on your doing certain things, whereby you are of use to me; and the good I am prepared to do you is proportional to your value to me. In the terminology of the Theory of Games, we form a coalition, because we each see that together we can achieve some of our respective interests better than we could separately. But our assessment of the outcome remains separate. Your good is not

---

[8] John Lucas, *Freedom and Grace* (London, 1976), 56.

eo ipso my good, and your value in my eyes is simply as a person who can bring good things to me, as a furtherer of my own cause. Anybody else who could do the same would do equally well. I have no commitments to you as you, but only to you as a useful business partner.[9]

In love, however, I further your true interests because through identification they have become my own. In this way you and the realization of your true interests have acquired *intrinsic value* for me. For me you cannot be replaced by anybody else. You are for me, in the words of Immanuel Kant,[10] an end in yourself ('Zweck an sich selbst') with unconditional value and not something, which only has value for me on condition that it is useful for furthering my interests.

By thus identifying with each other in love, we bestow on each other a unique value as irreplaceable and indispensable individuals:

> If you are accepted because you are you, not only is your value in my eyes not conditional and not necessarily limited, but it is also unique. I can do business with anybody, but if I have a personal relationship with you, and value you because you are you, I cannot have *that* relationship with anybody else, just simply because anybody else is not you.[11]

In brief, we are not only dependent on the recognition of others for our identity as persons but our value as persons is also determined by their identification with us:

> To be esteemed by another secures one's own self-esteem, and gives body to one's own sense of identity. To know that one is loved is to be able to anchor one's own existence in the affections of others. 'Who am I?' 'I am the person that Mother loves' or 'that Jill loves' or 'that God loves'. It means that my actions matter, not only to me but to someone else in the outside world, and that therefore they have a significance which is not solely solipsistic.[12]

A third characteristic of such relationships is that they can only be established and maintained in mutual freedom. Love cannot be earned or coerced. Jean-Paul Sartre[13] points out that someone who longs to be loved does not want to turn his beloved into his slave. He does not want to become the object of a passion flowing forth mechanically from his beloved. He does not want to possess an automaton and, if we want to humiliate him, we need only try to persuade him that his beloved's passion is not freely bestowed on him but is the effect of a psychological determinism. The lover will then feel that both his love and his being are cheapened. If the beloved is transformed into an automaton, the lover finds himself alone. This is well illustrated in the popular song 'Paper Doll':

---

[9] Lucas, *Freedom and Grace*, 57. On this point see also J.A. Brook, 'How to treat persons as persons', in A. Montefiore (ed.), *Philosophy and Personal Relations* (London, 1973), 66, and Van de Vate, *Romantic Love*, 19f.

[10] See section two of Kant's *Fundamental Principles of the Metaphysics of Ethics* (London, 1959).

[11] Lucas, *Freedom and Grace*, 58.

[12] Lucas, *Freedom and Grace*, 60.

[13] Jean-Paul Sartre, *Being and Nothingness*, 367.

I'm goin' to buy a paper doll that I can call my own,
A doll that other fellows cannot steal.
And then those flirty flirty guys
With their flirty flirty eyes
Will have to flirt with dollies that are real.
When I come home at night she will be waiting.
She'll be the truest doll in all the world.
I'd rather have a paper doll to call my own
Than have a fickle minded real live girl.

Far from being a love song, this is a lament on the absence of love. In the words of Sartre, 'If the beloved is transformed into an automaton, the lover finds himself alone' – alone with his paper doll. It is clear that a relationship of love can only be maintained as long as the personal integrity and free autonomy of *both* partners is maintained. As soon as I try to control you as an object or allow you to treat me as an object, our relationship is perverted into something other than love. Love must by its very nature be a relationship of free mutual give and take, otherwise it cannot be love at all.

This voluntary nature of love suggests a fourth characteristic, namely its vulnerability. If I cannot force or oblige you to return my love, I remain dependent in relation to you. A relationship of love is therefore vulnerable since it depends for its initiation as well as its maintenance on the freedom and the dependability of both partners. This vulnerability causes doubt, uncertainty and suffering in the lovers because of the tension between the desire to be loved and the inability to bring this about. This tension often becomes unbearable with the result that we are tempted to coerce or oblige our partners to return our love. By giving in to this temptation, the quality of our loving identification with each other is seriously impaired. I no longer seek to serve your interests purely because I have made them my own, but also in order to oblige or even coerce you to serve my interests in return. In many subtle ways I try to earn your love and your services or somehow to *make* you commit yourself to me. In this way I fail to treat you consistently as a person, and you often become for me an object that I somehow seek to control. Because of our fallibility and finitude, our human love is therefore rarely pure.

This raises a fifth characteristic of love: it is a relationship between *persons*. Here personhood has two sides to it. On the one hand, a person is a being who is treated in a personal way. I am a person to the extent that others treat me as a person and do not use me as an object, as an end in myself and not as a means to be used for some further end. Here Martin Buber[14] distinguishes two fundamental attitudes we adopt in relation to our environment: 'I-thou' and 'I-it'. Persons differ from objects because we adopt an 'I-thou' attitude towards them and not the 'I-it' attitude we adopt towards objects. So, too, P.F. Strawson distinguishes the attitude constitutive for personal

---

[14] Martin Buber, *I and Thou* (Edinburgh, 1952).

relations from the 'objective attitude' in which we treat something as an object. 'To adopt the objective attitude to another human being is to see him, perhaps, as an object of social policy; as a subject of what, in a wide range of sense, might be called treatment; as something ... to be managed or handled or cured or trained.'[15] Although we can adopt an objective attitude towards all entities (including people) by treating or controlling them as objects, we cannot adopt a personal attitude towards all entities. Only free agents, who as moral beings are able to initiate and bear responsibility for their own actions, can be approached as persons. This also entails that persons are self-conscious rational beings because these characteristics are a necessary condition for purposive and responsible agency. Although persons are, on the one hand, the intentional objects of a personal attitude, they are, on the other hand, also the bearers of all those personal characteristics that are the necessary condition for being approached as persons. In approaching someone as a person, I therefore presuppose that he or she is the bearer of these characteristics. Only with persons in this double sense can we establish a personal relationship in which we, in mutual freedom, can identify with each other in love and assume responsibility for each other's true interests.

As we have shown, Augustine and Bernard claim that ultimate happiness consists in enjoying a personal relationship of loving fellowship with God. It is now clear that this claim presupposes that not only we humans but also God must be a personal being. We are to approach God as a person and not as an object, as a 'thou' and not as an 'it'. We also presuppose that God is the bearer of those personal characteristics required in a personal relationship: God is a free and self-conscious agent who identifies with us in love and desires that we should enjoy the ultimate happiness of a loving relationship with him.

Divine Love

God must therefore be a person for those who believe that ultimate happiness consists in enjoying the loving fellowship of God. And yet, God is not like other people. Unlike us, finite humans as we are, God is unlimited in his goodness, knowledge, power and faithfulness. This has important consequences not only for the nature of his personhood, but also for the nature of the personal relationship of love we might enjoy with him. As persons we are finite and limited in our relations with each other and also in our relations with God. God, however, is infinite and free from the limitations of our human condition. This does not mean, however, that God is an impersonal being. On the contrary, as infinite and perfect being, he is also perfect in his personhood. With an impersonal God, we cannot enjoy a personal relationship of love nor can we find our ultimate happiness in his love. Only with a personal God who is also free from the limitations of our human condition, can we find that perfect

---

[15] P.F. Strawson, *Freedom and Resentment and Other Essays* (London, 1974), 9.

fellowship of love the enjoyment of which is ultimate happiness. Let me explain this in the light of three fundamental differences between God and ourselves and the implications that these differences have for the kind of relationship that we might have with God.

The first crucial difference is the following. Love between humans entails that by mutual identification each partner makes the interests of the other his or her own. However, the interests of my beloved are not necessarily identical with his or her wishes and will for the same reason that my interests are not necessarily in accordance with my wishes and will. As humans we are fallible and weak, and consciously or unconsciously we often will things that are not good for us and not in accordance with our true interests. Therefore, love between humans does not necessarily require that I always grant my beloved what he or she wills, but only that I should try to serve the *true* interests of my beloved as I honestly but fallibly understand these to be. Of course, this does not mean that I am indifferent to the will and wishes of my beloved. In my practical deliberations I will always take the wishes and will of my beloved into account, but this does not mean that I will always automatically grant these. The wishes and will of my beloved always remain fallible in the same way as my own wishes and will remain fallible.

In contrast to our human will, the will of God is perfect and infallibly good. In fact, for believers the will of God counts as the ultimate standard of goodness. To do the will of God *is* to do what is good. Our love for God is therefore our identification with his perfect will. It is only when through love we have made God's will our own, that we can find ultimate happiness in a life in accordance with his will. This suggests an essential requirement for ultimate happiness: it can only be achieved when as persons we realize our *true* interests and these consist in realizing the ultimate good in our individual lives. In the words of Augustine, quoted above, 'No one can be happy who does not enjoy what is man's chief good, not is there anyone who enjoys this who is not happy.' For Augustine the chief end of human existence is to do the will of God, since to do that *is* to do what is ultimately good. This was one of the main reasons why things went so horribly wrong for the prodigal son: he tried to find happiness in achieving finite goods rather than in seeking what is ultimately good. He was therefore fundamentally mistaken about the nature of his *true* interests.

This does not mean, however, that in seeking to do the will of God we always do so out of love and not merely out of duty. When we do the will of God out of duty, we experience it as an external law imposed on us from outside and not as something that through the identification of love has become our own. Then the 'good life' can be for us no more than being virtuous out of duty instead of doing the will of God out of love. We then do the will of God because we ought to and not because we find our ultimate happiness in doing it. This suggests a further essential requirement for ultimate happiness: to be ultimately happy it is not enough to do what is ultimately good in our individual lives. We should also do so authentically because we choose it with integrity. Realizing the good in our individual lives as a duty imposed on us from outside cannot make us ultimately happy. Sartre is right in his claim that we should choose our individual identity with integrity and not allow it to be imposed on us from outside. But then we can only be happy when we do the will of God out of love and not merely out of duty.

A second relevant difference between God and ourselves is related to the limits of our human knowledge and capacities, which in turn sets limits to the range and intensity with which we can identify with others. Thus 'real friendship takes time and energy which human beings have in limited amounts. We cannot have too many friends for the same reason as we cannot do too much work. We cannot spread ourselves too thin.'[16] Apart from such restrictions of time and energy, it is especially the limits of our knowledge of others, which determines the range and intensity of our fellowship with them. I can only identify with your good to the extent that I know what your good is, and I can only take your feelings, desires, intentions, dispositions, values, preferences, character and so on into account in my own practical reasoning to the extent that these are known to me. For this reason 'love cannot do without information. The lover is relentlessly curious as to his beloved's sorrows, joys, and desires, which concern him as his own.'[17] There is a limit to the number of people whom we can come to know and the amount of knowledge we can acquire about them. There is also a limit to the number of people with whom we can achieve real fellowship and great differences in the intensity of the fellowship we are able to establish and maintain with different people. We know very few people well enough to identify with them intensively, and even our knowledge of our nearest and dearest is finite and fallible. We can be mistaken about the true interests of others in the same way as we can be mistaken about our own. We know very little about most people with whom we interact in life, and the few things we do know about them, we also find in others. Hence, they remain for us not much more than comparable bearers of those properties that they share with others and, as such, are replaceable by those with the same properties. It is therefore difficult for us to treat them consistently as irreplaceable persons. They are for us no more than partners in a tacit agreement of rights and obligations in which they become for us mere replaceable means for serving our own ends.

For believers this is different in their relationship with God. For God all hearts lie open, all desires are known and no secrets are hidden. God cannot be mistaken about our true interests, and since all our feelings, desires, intentions, dispositions and so on are fully known to him, he can infallibly take them into account in his dealings with us. Since God knows every one of us fully, he need not treat us as though we were all equal in his sight and therefore able to replace each other in his affection: 'No human being is worth less than another in God's sight, not because they are all worth the same, but because each one is irreplaceable.'[18] In this way God's love for us is not impartial but partial in the sense in which 'partiality is a matter of looking to see what

---

[16] Helen Oppenheimer, *The Hope of Happiness* (London, 1983), 136. Cf. Emil Brunner's statement that 'a person who claims friendship with everyone has not begun to understand the meaning of friendship', in *The Divine Imperative* (London, 1949), 518.

[17] Roger Scruton, *Sexual Desire* (London, 1986), 231.

[18] Oppenheimer, *The Hope of Happiness*, 81.

the special individuality of the other person really is and attending positively to it. God can have this kind of special love for each of his creatures.'[19] Elsewhere Helen Oppenheimer expands this point as follows:

> God loves each creature: but even 'each' is still too abstract here, and to bring out the full sense one must risk the subjective, 'God loves *me*': not externally but with a 'partial' love which enters completely and as of right into my unique point of view ... God abides in me in this sense, that he associates himself to the point of identification with the pettiness as well as the glory of every creature he has made ... To form the idea that God is the 'ground of one's being' in the sense that he is more concerned for one, more 'partial' to one, more on one's side, than one is oneself; that one's humanly private point of view is so to say anchored onto the divine: is assuredly to feel that one has 'got more than one bargained for'.[20]

In this way God's love is 'partial' to every single one of us.

Nicholas of Cusa[21] illustrated this 'universal partiality' of God's love graphically with reference to the kind of portrait paintings in which the person in the painting looks the onlooker straight in the eye. A well-known example would be Leonardo da Vinci's *Mona Lisa*. If you stand before the *Mona Lisa*, she looks straight at you in a way that makes you feel that you are the only person in the world to whom she is attending. If you move over to the right or to the left, she will still be looking at you like that. It is as if her eyes follow you wherever you go. However, if I were to look at her from the right and you from the left, she would look at each of us separately as if each of us were the only one to whom she was attending! Because of this effect, Nicholas calls this kind of portrait painting an 'icon of God': God looks on each of us *individually* since each one of us is irreplaceable in his sight. By contrast, the Pope on his balcony looks inclusively at the whole crowd of people on St Peter's Square without looking at anyone in particular. God's love, however, is both inclusive and exclusive at the same time. For believers God alone knows each one of us well enough to be able to identify with the true personal interests of each of us individually. God alone is able to treat each one of us individually as a person, as a 'thou'. In this respect, too, God is perfect as a Person and free from the limitations of our finite personhood. This suggests an important reason why ultimate happiness can only be found in the love of God: God alone knows me well enough to consistently treat me as an irreplaceable individual and hence to bestow individual identity and value on me as a person. Only in the eyes of God can I ultimately be 'famous'.

A third relevant difference between God and us has to do with God's immutable faithfulness. If I love you, I commit myself to serving your true interests as being my own. In this way, serving your interests becomes part of my chosen identity as a person. It is incorporated into the ideals I strive to realize in my life and in which I find my identity. However, this is only possible as long as my chosen identity remains

---

[19] Oppenheimer, *The Hope of Happiness*, 135.

[20] Helen Oppenheimer, *Incarnation and Immanence* (London, 1973), 191–2.

[21] Nicholas of Cusa, *The Vision of God* (New York, 1969), 3f.

compatible with serving your interests. As humans, however, we are not only able to become unfaithful to each other and to our identification with each other, but the circumstances of our lives could give rise to changes in our chosen identity which make it difficult for us to continue to identify with each other. Our chosen identity as persons is not immutably stable. Thus you may change in the course of time in ways which make it increasingly difficult for me to identify with you with integrity. Or I myself may change in ways that prevent me from continuing to identify with you as before. Lovers and friends can grow apart in the course of time. According to Ortega y Gasset such changes in personal identity are normal and naturally give rise to changes in our amorous commitments:

> This is the normal case. A personality experiences in the course of its life two or three great transformations, which are like different stages of the same moral trajectory. Without losing solidarity, or even the fundamental homogeneity of yesterday's feelings, we notice one day that we have entered upon a new phase or modulation of our characters … Our innermost being seems, in each one of these two or three phases, to rotate a few degrees upon its axis, to shift towards another quadrant of the universe and to orient itself towards new constellations. Is it not a meaningful coincidence that the number of true loves which the normal man usually experiences is almost always the same in number: two or three? And, moreover, that each of these loves appears chronologically localized in each of these stages in character?[22]

Ortega is right that people can change in this way. However, he is wrong in thinking that such changes simply happen to us and are beyond our control. Changes in our personal identity do not follow with unavoidable necessity from changes in the circumstances of our lives, but they do result from the ways in which we decide to respond to such changes. If lovers respond to changing circumstances in ways that are incompatible, they will grow apart. If, however, they seek to respond in ways that are compatible, their personal identities will change and develop in concert, and they will grow together in the course of time. In this sense a relationship of love or fellowship is a joint venture. In the long run it can only be maintained to the extent that both partners commit themselves to it and manage to grow together with integrity in the ways in which they respond to changes in the circumstances of their lives. However, the partners in such a relationship can never have any cast-iron guarantee that neither of them will ever change in ways that might lead them to grow apart. Not only do fair-weather friends let each other down, as the prodigal son discovered to his distress. Real friends and lovers also remain finite and fallible in their commitments to each other. In this way our human love always remains risky and vulnerable. Not only can lovers fail to maintain their loving identification with each other, but also, as we have argued in the previous section, the quality of their mutual identification remains finite and impure. I try to limit the risk of losing you against my will by somehow coercing or obliging you to maintain your identification with me.

---

[22] José Ortega y Gasset, *On Love. Aspects of a Single Theme* (London, 1959), 82–3.

In this respect, too, God is not like other people. Love of God is not risky like human love since we cannot only count on God to remain faithful to his character, but his character is also stable and unlike ours it does not change. Hence, believers would claim that estrangement from God could never result from God changing and growing apart from us, but only from our becoming unfaithful to God and turning our backs on him. In the words of Augustine: 'No one can lose you, my God, unless he forsakes you.'[23] This suggests a further reason why *ultimate* happiness can only be found in the love of God. No one will deny that we can anchor our identity and self-esteem in the affections of others and hence that we can find happiness in human fellowship and love. Nevertheless, human love remains finite and fallible. Since God's love is eternally dependable, we can never lose it against our will. For this reason believers claim that the love of God is the only eternally dependable anchor for our ultimate happiness.

Unhappiness and Estrangement from God

Let me recapitulate. I have argued that to be ultimately happy, I must be both 'rich' and 'famous'. I am rich when I come to know and have the means, the ability and the opportunity to realize my daimon, that is, my individual potentiality to achieve the Good in my life. My daimon constitutes my personal identity as an individual and makes me to be the person I am. In realizing my daimon I achieve ultimate fulfilment as a person. However, being 'rich' in this sense is not enough. To be ultimately happy I must also be 'famous' in the sense that my personal ideals are endorsed and my chosen identity is recognized and appreciated by others. I need others to recognize that my individual good is part of their own and therefore to share responsibility with me for realizing this in my life.

According to the Christian tradition we can only become 'rich and famous' in this sense when we enjoy the loving fellowship of God. I am 'rich' when I love God and identify with him by making his will my own. Doing the will of God *is* to do what is Good and realizing God's will for me as a person *is* to realize my daimon. I am 'famous' when God loves me with a 'partial' love and identifies with me personally by making my ultimate happiness his very own concern. In that case, he will make his will for me known to me and provide me with the means, the capacities and the opportunities to realize this in my life. In loving me, God enables me to return his love and thus to be blessed with ultimate happiness: 'When God loves, he desires nothing but to be loved, since he loves us for no other reason than to be loved, for he knows that those who love him are blessed in their very love.'[24]

This is the ideal. In practice, however, we humans fail to realize this ideal more than partially and imperfectly, if at all. The result is that ultimate happiness eludes us

---

[23] Augustine, *Confessions*, IV.8.

[24] Bernard of Clairvaux, *Sermons on the Song of Songs* (4 vols, Kalamazoo, MI, 1971–80), sermon 83.

and we remain unhappy in life because we become estranged from God. We fail to identify with God in love by making his will our own. The result is that the will of God remains for us no more than an external duty that we fulfil because we must and not because we want to. We are therefore unable to choose authentically to do the will of God. Like the prodigal son we leave the Father's house and go to a distant country where we try to 'do our own thing'. Like him we seek our 'riches' by striving after finite goods and in doing so we rely on our finite knowledge, our finite means, our finite capacities and our finite opportunities. Like the prodigal son, we end up in frustration because things often do not pan out as we had hoped. Furthermore, we seek our 'fame' in the recognition and support of finite persons who more often than not can let us down. We seek our riches and fame in finite goods that, as Augustine points out, 'can be lost against the will'. And this can never provide us with ultimate happiness since 'no one can feel confident regarding a good which he knows can be taken from him, although he wishes to keep and cherish it. But if a man feels no confidence regarding the good that he enjoys, how can he be happy while in such fear of losing it?' (*De Moribus* 3.5). From this, as we have seen, Augustine concludes that 'our chief good, that we must hasten to arrive at in preference to all other things is nothing else than God'. Since nothing can separate us from his love, this must be 'surer as well as better than any other good' (*De Moribus* 11.18).

It is here that we have to ask ourselves how we can be reconciled with the God from whom we have become estranged. Let us therefore now first consider how human persons become estranged from each other and what is required for them to be reconciled, and then see to what extent reconciliation with God can be understood as analogous to such human reconciliation.

Estrangement and Reconciliation

Estrangement

We have argued that loving fellowship is a relationship in which two persons identify with each other by each making the other's real interests his or her own. In thus serving your interests not merely in the same way that I serve my own, but as *being* my own, I love you as myself. If all people were to love both God and each other in this way, we would have peace on earth and the Kingdom of God would be with us! Unfortunately this ideal is far from being realized in the broken world in which we live. Because of our finitude and fallibility most people remain forever strangers to us, and even those fellowships which we do achieve in life remain fragile and under the constant threat of estrangement.

We can only make the real interests of others our own to the extent that we know what these are. Since the vast majority of those who cross our path are strangers about whom we know nothing, we can hardly identify with them in fellowship. Since we do not know what their interests are, we cannot make these our own. Often we tend to adopt what Sartre calls an 'attitude of indifference' toward them:

> We are dealing with a kind of blindness toward others ... I practice then a sort of factual solipsism; others are those forms that pass by in the street, those magic objects which are capable of acting at a distance and upon which I can act by means of determined conduct. I scarcely notice them; I act as if I were alone in the world. I brush against 'people' as I brush against a wall; I avoid them as I avoid obstacles ... I do not even imagine that they can look at me. Of course they have some knowledge of me, but this knowledge does not touch me. It is a question of pure modifications of their being that ... express what they are, not what I am and they are the effect of my actions upon them. Those 'people' are functions: the ticket collector is only the function of collecting tickets; the café waiter is nothing but the function of serving patrons. In this capacity they will be most useful if I knew their *keys* and those 'master-words' that can release their mechanisms.[1]

In this way we come to treat other people not as persons but as objects that we either ignore or use to serve our own interests. In order to use them, we only need to know the 'master-words that can release their mechanisms'. We do not serve their interests but look on them as means to serve our own. When they fail to do so to our satisfaction, we might 'act [upon them] by means of determined conduct' and pressurize them in various ways to perform better, or else we could merely replace them with other means that serve our purposes better. They are dispensable and replaceable objects that we try to manipulate in our own interest.

---

[1] Jean-Paul Sartre, *Being and Nothingness* (New York, 1956), 380–81.

It might be objected that we are not completely ignorant about the interests of the stranger. After all, there are various basic human needs such as food, clothing, shelter, security, and so on that all people have in common. It is therefore always possible for us to serve these interests of a stranger rather than treating him or her merely as an object that we use to serve our own. True as this is, it does not mean that in serving the interests of strangers we also have loving fellowship with them. Our attitude towards them can be one of beneficent care by which (in the words of Strawson quoted in the previous chapter) we see the stranger 'as a subject of ... treatment ... to be managed or handled or cured or trained'. Beneficence does not necessarily entail treating the other as a person rather than as an object. It is clear that, although loving fellowship is impossible without serving the interests of the other, it is much more than mere beneficence. In 1 Corinthians 13:3 St Paul suggests that even when my beneficence should extend to giving away all I possess to the needy and giving up my body to be burned, it remains possible that in doing this I have no love.

John Macmurray argues this point as follows:

> If in my relation with you I insist on behaving generously toward you and refuse to accept your generosity in return, I make myself the giver and you the recipient. This is unjust to you. I put you in my debt and refuse to let you repay the debt. In that case I make the relation an unequal one. You are to have continual cause to be grateful to me, but I am not to be grateful to you. This is the worst kind of tyranny, and is shockingly unfair to you. It destroys the mutuality of the personal by destroying the equality that is its negative aspect. To maintain equality of persons in relation is justice; and without it generosity becomes purely sentimental and wholly egocentric. My care for you is only moral if it includes the intention to preserve your freedom as an agent which is your independence of me. Even if you wish to be dependent on me, it is my business, for your sake, to prevent it.[2]

Of course, generosity is not always in this way unfair to the recipient. On the contrary, there is nothing wrong in giving generously to organizations that feed the hungry in the Third World. In that case, however, the recipient of my generosity remains anonymous and is unable to respond. The same applies to the care of those who are in some way mentally or physically unable to respond in the mutuality of the personal. Here generosity or beneficent care does not destroy the mutuality of the personal because such mutuality is excluded in any case. However, this does not contradict the important point that loving fellowship is necessarily a mutual personal relationship and as such it is perverted when it is purposely reduced to mere beneficent care.

Not all our relations with other people become impersonal in these ways. We also manage to maintain the mutuality of the personal in our relations with other people. This does not mean, however, that all our personal relations are relations of loving fellowship. Very often our relations with others are no more that the tacit agreements of rights and obligations which we described in the previous chapter. I serve your interests in order that you should serve mine in return. I do not serve your interests as

---

[2] John Macmurray, *Persons in Relation* (London, 1961), 189–90.

my own but only with a view to earning your services. I take on the obligation to serve you in order to earn the right to your serving me.

Such tacit agreements come to grief when one of us fails to fulfil his or her obligations towards the other. When I damage your interests by not serving them in the way I am obliged to do under the tacit agreement, you can respond in various ways. You might decide to dispense with my services and find somebody else who can serve your interests better. After all, you are not interested in me but only in my services. I am therefore not indispensable to you as I would be in a relationship of loving fellowship. On the other hand, you might decide to patch up our relationship in some way by trying to restore the balance of rights and obligations that I have violated. This can be done in three ways. First, you could count the costs and decide that the damage I did to your interests is not serious enough for you to break with me completely. You can then merely overlook what I have done or condone it under the circumstances in the hope that I will fulfil my obligations to you better in future. On the other hand, you might decide that the damage I did to you is too serious to condone. You therefore demand satisfaction from me. I either have as yet to fulfil my obligations to your satisfaction or I have to provide you with an alternative service to make up for the damage I did you. If for some reason I am unable to give you the required satisfaction, I might try to get someone else to do so in my stead. After all, you are not interested in me but only in my services, and therefore it does not matter to you whether it is I or someone else in my stead that provides them as long as your interests are served in the way we have agreed. If, however, I am neither able to give you satisfaction nor get someone else to do so in my stead, you can restore the balance of rights and obligations between us by punishing me. Thus you could either withhold your services to me to the same extent that I have failed to serve you, or you can damage my interests to the same extent that I have damaged yours. You could 'make the punishment fit the crime'. Thus by condonation or satisfaction or punishment the balance of rights and obligations between us can be restored to the way it was before I failed to fulfil my obligations to you as I should have under the tacit agreement between us.

As we have argued in the previous chapter, loving fellowship is a very different kind of personal relationship than tacit agreements of rights and obligations. It demands far more from us to maintain such fellowship. Owing to human weakness, we are all too often unable to sustain this sort of fellowship consistently. Through thoughtlessness or selfishness I fail to consistently make your interests my own. I seek my own interests above yours, and intentionally or unintentionally act in ways that are contrary to your interests and thus cause you injury. Irrespective of whether the injury is serious or trivial, I have damaged our fellowship and given you grounds for resentment. In being resentful, you endorse the fact that our fellowship has been damaged, if not destroyed, and that we have therefore become estranged. Overcoming such estrangement requires much more than merely restoring the balance of rights and obligations between us. Here we need to achieve personal reconciliation. How is this to be achieved?

Reconciliation

Such estrangement can only be overcome if you refuse to be resentful, and instead adopt the opposite attitude, that is, willingness to forgive. You have to consider the breach in our relationship a greater evil than the injury I have caused you, and therefore be willing to continue identifying with me and treating my interests as your own in spite of what I have done to you: 'The person who has been wronged can accept the wrong done to him: he can absorb as it were in his own suffering the consequences of the wrong that has caused it.'[3]

Such forgiveness can only be both real and effective on certain conditions. Thus it can only be *real* if there is something to forgive. It would make no sense to say that you forgive me unless I really caused you injury by failing to seek your interests as my own. Herein lies the difference between forgiveness and condonation. If you were to *condone* my action, you would thereby *deny* that it is an action that caused you real injury, and thus also deny that there is anything to forgive. If, on the other hand, you *forgive* me for what I have done, you claim that my action did cause you injury, but that you would rather bear the injury than abandon the fellowship that I have damaged by my action. Forgiveness entails that, for the sake of reconciliation, you give up your right to pay me back in my own coin by demanding satisfaction or by punishing me: 'The power to forgive is not to be obtained for nothing, it must be bought at a price, it must be paid for with the suffering of him who has been sinned against.'[4] One of the fundamental characteristics of forgiveness is therefore that 'the one who forgives is the one who suffers'.[5] Thus forgiveness costs you something, whereas condonation is a denial that there are any serious costs involved.[6]

Your forgiveness can only be *effective* in restoring our broken fellowship, on condition that I am sincerely penitent and express both contrition for damaging our fellowship and the desire that it should be restored. Loving fellowship is a two-way affair that cannot be one-sidedly established, maintained or restored. Hence there are two necessary conditions for reconciliation: forgiveness on your part and penitence and a change of heart on mine. Forgiveness alone is not enough. It is your willingness to identify with me in spite of what I did. But if I do not through penitence renounce the damage that I have done our fellowship and express my change of heart, your identification with me would not restore the relationship but rather entail your acquiescence in my breaking of it. It follows that if I sincerely desire reconciliation and therefore ask your forgiveness, this *entails* penitence and a change of heart on my

---

[3] John Burnaby, *Christian Words and Christian Meanings* (London, 1955), 90.

[4] O.C. Quick, *Essays in Orthodoxy* (London, 1916), 92–3.

[5] J. Edwin Orr, *Full Surrender* (Edinburgh, 1951), 22.

[6] For a more detailed analysis of the differences between forgiveness and condonation, see R.S. Downie, 'Forgiveness', *Philosophical Quarterly*, 15 (1965). See also Lucas, *Freedom and Grace*, 78f. An example of someone who interprets forgiveness in terms of condonation or pardon, is A. Alhonsaari, *Prayer. An Analysis of Theological Terminology* (Helsinki, 1973), 161f.

part as well as the expression of these in penitential action.[7] The one would be incoherent without the other:

> To ask to be forgiven is in part to acknowledge that the attitude displayed in our actions was such as might properly be resented and in part to repudiate that attitude for the future (or at least for the immediate future); and to forgive is to accept the repudiation and to forswear the resentment.[8]

In this way asking forgiveness is very different from asking for condonation. The latter entails the claim that what I have done is not as bad as it seems and does not require a change of heart on my part.

Although my penitence is in this sense a necessary condition for your forgiveness to be effective in restoring our fellowship, it is not a condition for your forgiveness as such. Like love itself, forgiveness is unconditional and can only be freely given. It follows that my penitence can neither cause nor earn your forgiveness. Whether you are to identify with me again depends on your freely deciding to do so. It takes two to repair personal fellowship just as it takes two to establish it in the first place. Forgiveness can only be freely given, and when it is forced or earned it ceases to be forgiveness. My penance and my attempts to make good the injury I have caused you cannot be more than an expression of my penitence or an attempt to put into practice my repudiation of what I have done. They can neither bring about nor earn your forgiveness since that remains up to you to decide. This is what distinguishes penitence and penance from punishment and satisfaction. Through bearing punishment or making satisfaction I can *earn* reinstatement in a relationship of rights and obligations, and what I have earned you are obliged to give. Penitence and penance, however, can never *earn* reinstatement in a relation of fellowship, and therefore cannot in the same way create obligations. Furthermore, although penitence and penance are a necessary condition for forgiveness to be effective, punishment and satisfaction would make forgiveness unnecessary. If full satisfaction has been made or appropriate punishment has been borne, there is nothing left to forgive: 'Forgiveness after satisfaction has been fully made, is no forgiveness at all.'[9] Thus I can never *demand* your forgiveness as a right that I have earned. I can only *ask* it as a favour. In asking your forgiveness (as in asking you anything else) I acknowledge my dependence on your free decision for granting my request. I may hope that you will forgive. I might even count on you to forgive me when I am penitent. But my penitence does not entitle me to your forgiveness and therefore I may not presume upon it.

Like forgiveness, penitence and penance should also be free and unconditional. If you have harmed or abused me and thus failed to maintain our fellowship, I cannot

---

[7] 'Etymologically, of course, there is no difference between penance and penitence; both come from the same Latin source, *poenitentia*, but the existence of the two words in English makes it possible for us to distinguish between penitence, as an inner state, and penance, as a manifestation of it in action' (H.A. Hodges, *The Pattern of Atonement* [London, 1955], 54).

[8] P.F. Strawson, *Freedom and Resentments and Other Essays* (London, 1974), 6.

[9] G.W.H. Lampe, 'The atonement: law and love', in A.R. Vidler, *Soundings* (Cambridge, 1966), 185.

force you to be penitent and be reconciled with me. A change of heart on your part must necessarily be free. If, however, I sincerely desire reconciliation with you and therefore forgive you for what you have done to me, this entails that I also want you to seek reconciliation with me and therefore repudiate what you have done to me and through a change of heart identify with me again. Although I cannot force you to repudiate, I can do my best to persuade you freely to do so. If I were to forgive you without desiring your repentance and urging you to have a change of heart, my forgiveness would merely confirm you in the role as my abuser and myself in the role as your victim. My forgiveness expresses my desire to be reconciled with you despite what you have done to me, and not my acquiescence in your continuing to do so and thus to continue to undermine our fellowship. Such acquiescence would leave everything as it is and cannot lead to reconciliation.

If I repudiate the damage I have done to our fellowship by confessing myself in the wrong and by an act of penance try to demonstrate my change of heart and the sincerity of this repudiation, and if I express my desire for the restoration of our fellowship by asking your forgiveness, and if you, by forgiving me, show your willingness to identify with me again, then our fellowship will not only be restored, but might also be deepened and strengthened:

> We shall be to one another what we were before, save for one important difference. I know now that you are a person who can forgive, that you prefer to have suffered rather than to resent, and that to keep me as a friend, or to avoid becoming my enemy, is more important to you than to maintain your own rights. And you know that I am a person who is not too proud to acknowledge his fault, and that your goodwill is worth more to me than the maintenance of my own cause ... Forgiveness does not only forestall or remove enmity: it strengthens love.[10]

In sum, whereas broken fellowship can only be restored by penitence and forgiveness, broken agreements of rights and obligations are restored by satisfaction or by punishment or by condonation. If we do not clearly distinguish fellowship from a tacit agreement of rights and obligations, we will also tend to confuse penitence and penance with satisfaction or punishment, and forgiveness with condonation.

The Price of Reconciliation

Reconciliation is not easy. It comes at a price. Reconciliation is impossible without penitence and a change of heart on the part of the one who damaged the fellowship, and forgiveness on the part of the injured party. Since both penitence and forgiveness are not easy or cheap, we are reluctant to pay the price for reconciliation.

If I have wronged you, I have to be willing to admit that I was wrong and show remorse for what I did to you. This involves a change of heart in which I amend my

---

[10] Burnaby, *Christian Words and Christian Meanings*, 87.

identity as a person in relation to you. I must renounce the 'I' who has wronged you and again become the 'I' who identifies with you and seeks your interests as being my own. I also have to demonstrate this change of heart through some form of penance showing that I am serious about seeking your interests as my own. Furthermore I have to admit anew that I am dependent on your freedom and favour for restoring and maintaining the fellowship between us. I must admit that I do not earn or deserve your forgiveness but can only receive it from you with gratitude as a free gift. In fact I must show that restoring my fellowship with you is more important to me than the price of penitence and penance required from me as condition for reconciliation.

For all of us this is a high price to pay. I am too proud to admit that I have wronged you. Change of heart affects my sense of identity and undermines my self-confidence. Having to admit my dependence on your favour for restoring and maintaining our fellowship means having to accept my vulnerability in relation to you. I do not control our relationship. This also makes me uncertain about myself. Finally, I remain too selfish to treat your interests consistently as my own and will always in the long run tend to revert to my old 'I' who seeks my own interest above all else.

For all these reasons I will do my best to think up reasons which mitigate what I have done to you and thus lower the price of penitence and penance that I have to pay. I will try to show that what I did to you was not as bad as it sounds and therefore should not harm our fellowship too much. Hence you might as well overlook or condone what I did and let us continue as before. Or I will claim that I did not know that my actions would cause you so much harm. What I did was unfortunate but was done unintentionally and is therefore not blameworthy. Or else I will argue that under the circumstances I could not avoid harming your interests but this should be blamed on the circumstances and not on me. Or I could argue that, although what I did to you caused you harm, it was only what everybody (including you) would have done under the circumstances. I may be blameworthy, but not uniquely so. To err is human, and I am only human. Or else I could appeal to the fact that when people quarrel it is rarely the case that only one party is to blame. Therefore you have to share the blame with me for our estrangement. In brief, I will do my utmost to save face, because saving face is as important (if not more important) to me than to be reconciled with you.

It is clear that penitence and penance are not easy. But forgiveness is no less difficult. Let me illustrate this with two examples. In October 1944 the Dutch resistance killed two German soldiers in the town of Putten. As a reprisal, the Germans burned down part of the town and deported 588 men and boys to a concentration camp in Germany. Only 47 of these survived the war. Since then the incident is commemorated at an annual ceremony in Putten. In October 2000 the former SS soldier Albert Naumann, who was involved in the operation in 1944, attended the ceremony. According to the chairman E.H. De Graaf, the organizing committee had given Naumann permission to attend:

> It was a well-considered decision. We had discussed the matter and were unanimous that it would have violated our aim to contribute to reconciliation in

accordance with Holy Scripture, if we had forbidden him to attend. Naumann, by now an old man of 78, suffered from remorse for what he had done in the war, and that was not nothing. He had blood on his hands. We would have refused if he had been a SS soldier full of bravado who wanted to visit the important places of his youth. But now I shook the hand of an old man who was full of remorse for all the suffering he had caused.[11]

This handshake caused so much commotion in Putten that De Graaf and his committee had to resign.

My second example is from Archbishop Desmond Tutu, fighter against apartheid in South Africa, winner of the Nobel Peace Prize and chairman of the South African Truth and Reconciliation Commission. In his book *No Future without Forgiveness*, Tutu recounts the following incident:

> I had visited the Holy Land over Christmas 1989, and had the privilege, during my visit, of going to Yad Vashem, the Holocaust museum in Jerusalem. When the media asked me for my impressions, I told them it was a shattering experience. I added that the Lord whom I served, who was himself a Jew, would have asked, 'But what about forgiveness?' That remark set the cat among the pigeons. I was roundly condemned. I had also expressed my dismay at the treatment meted out to the Palestinians, which was in my view quite at variance with what the Jewish prophets taught and what the Jewish rabbi that we Christians followed demanded from his followers. I was charged with being anti-Semitic and graffiti appeared on the walls of St. George's Anglican Cathedral in Jerusalem, in whose close I was staying. It read, 'Tutu is a black Nazi pig'.[12]

These examples show how difficult it is to bring ourselves to forgive those who cause us pain or who damage our interests. The pain you caused me is too much for me to bear or to accept in order to forgive you. You have given me cause for resentment and I will rather nurse my resentment than to take leave of it and forgive you. Satisfaction and sweet revenge are more important to me than being reconciled with you and I am loath to give up my right to receive compensation and to see you adequately punished. I do not want to forgive you, and therefore I will do my best to think up reasons why I *cannot* forgive you, or even why I *may* not forgive you. I will convince myself that it would be morally wrong for me to do so. There are a number of arguments by which we usually try to show why we cannot or may not forgive.

Desmond Tutu recounts[13] how Simon Wiesenthal

> tells the story of how he was unable to forgive a Nazi soldier who asked to be forgiven. The soldier had been part of a group that rounded up a number of Jews, locked them up in a building and proceeded to set it alight, burning those inside to death. The soldier was now on his deathbed. His troubled conscience sought the relief that might come through unburdening himself, confessing his complicity

---

[11] This episode was reported in the Dutch newspaper *Trouw*, 27 October 2000.

[12] Desmond Tutu, *No Future without Forgiveness* (London 1999), 215–16.

[13] Tutu, *No Future without Forgiveness*, 222.

and getting absolution from a Jew. Simon listened to his terrible story in silence.
When the soldier had ended his narration, Simon left without uttering a word,
certainly not one of forgiveness. He asks at the end of his account, 'What would
you have done?'

I think that most of us would respond by admitting that we would have done the same.
According to Tutu,

> the dilemma Wiesenthal faced was very real. His own view, which seems to be
> that of many Jews, is that the living do not have the right to forgive on behalf of
> those who were killed, those who suffered in the past and are no longer alive to
> make the decision for themselves. One can understand their reluctance, since if
> they were to forgive it might appear they were trivializing the awful experience of
> the victims; it also might seem the height of presumption to speak on behalf of
> people who suffered so grievously. (Ibid.)

Wiesenthal puts forward two reasons for not forgiving the soldier. First, he argues that
the living have no right to forgive on behalf of the dead. On this point he is, of course,
quite right. I can only forgive the pain and suffering that has been inflicted on me
personally and not that which has been inflicted on somebody else. I can only
renounce my own resentment and not that of somebody else. The question is, however,
whether the soldier was asking Wiesenthal to forgive him on behalf of the victims. He
wanted 'absolution from a Jew' who was living and not from the victims who were
dead. He wanted Wiesenthal to give up his own resentment and forgive him. That was
what Wiesenthal could not bring himself to do and that is why he could not be
reconciled with the soldier. By his action towards the soldier, Wiesenthal merely
confirmed his *own* resentment and not his inability to give up the resentment of the
victims. Of course, the soldier could no longer be reconciled with his victims for they
were dead. He would just have to live with the fact that reconciliation with the dead is
impossible. But he could be reconciled with Wiesenthal the Jew, and that is what he
asked for. However, if he were a believer, he would not have been satisfied with that.
He would also have wanted divine forgiveness because his deeds not only gave cause
for resentment to Jews like Wiesenthal but to God as well. Therefore believers always
desire divine forgiveness for the suffering they cause each other. *Kyrie eleison.*

Wiesenthal's second argument was that forgiveness would trivialize the awful
experience of the victims. By forgiving you for what you have done to me, I say in
fact that what you have done was not so bad that I cannot live with it. In this way I
make light of the guilt you have incurred by what you have done to me. I fear that this
argument confuses forgiveness with condonation. As we have argued above, by
condoning what you have done I declare that it was not so bad and thereby that there
is really nothing serious to forgive. Condonation makes forgiveness unnecessary. By
forgiving you I fully acknowledge the pain you did to me, but declare that I would
rather bear the pain and give up my right to satisfaction than to abandon the
fellowship with you. As I have argued above, the one who forgives is the one who
pays the price. To pay the price is not to trivialize it.

A third argument we often use for not forgiving is an appeal to justice. Forgiveness, we say, is not possible unless justice is done. Since Wiesenthal devoted his whole life to seeking justice, it is clear that this consideration would also have been uppermost in his mind. Justice is the blindfolded lady holding up the scales in order to see to it that the balance of justice is restored. The question is, however, what kind of justice do we seek and what kind of balance do we want to restore? Usually we think of justice as bringing about a balance between sin and satisfaction, between guilt and punishment. Justice is done when the victim is adequately compensated and the perpetrator is adequately punished, when the punishment fits the crime. The victims, we say, have a right to adequate compensation and also to adequate punishment for the perpetrator. After the trail of the perpetrator the media invariably ask the victims whether they are satisfied with the verdict. Have they received that to which they as victims are entitled?

I fear that this kind of justice does not restore fellowship. In fact, the victim usually has no intention of being reconciled with the perpetrator and is only interested in compensation and in punishment for the perpetrator. This is retributive justice that sees to it that the perpetrator pays the price for his or her deeds, and makes it unnecessary for the victim to pay the price of forgiveness. Retribution makes forgiveness superfluous and does not restore fellowship. At most it can restore a tacit agreement of rights and obligations, on condition that the victim still desires such an agreement with the perpetrator. Usually the victims would prefer to have nothing to do with the perpetrator in future. If the victims have received their rights and consider the balance restored they are happy to terminate the relationship and, like Wiesenthal, turn their backs on the perpetrator.

Desmond Tutu argues that

> retributive justice … is not the only kind of justice. I contend that there is another kind of justice, restorative justice, which was characteristic of traditional African jurisprudence. Here the central concern is not retribution or punishment, but … the healing of breaches, the redressing of balances, the restoration of broken relationships. This kind of justice seeks to rehabilitate both the victim and the perpetrator, who should be given the opportunity to be reintegrated into the community he or she has injured by his or her offence. This is a much more personal approach, which sees the offence as something that has happened to people and whose consequence is a rupture in relationships. Thus we would claim that justice, restorative justice, is being served when efforts are being made to work for healing, for forgiveness and for reconciliation.[14]

It is clear therefore that forgiveness does not undermine the search for justice. But then we must seek the justice of reconciliation rather than that of retribution.

Even if in this way (retributive) justice is not a condition for forgiveness, we might argue that the repentance of the perpetrator is. Thus the so-called 'Kairos document', which contributed significantly to the South African debate on apartheid, argued that

---

[14] Tutu, *No Future without Forgiveness*, 51–2.

> no reconciliation, no forgiveness and no negotiations are possible *without repentance*. The Biblical teaching on reconciliation and forgiveness makes it quite clear that nobody can be forgiven and reconciled with God unless he or she repents of their sins. Nor are *we* expected to forgive the unrepentant sinner. When he or she repents we must be willing to forgive seventy times seven times but before that, we are expected to preach repentance to those who sin against us or against anyone else.[15]

This statement is correct on two points. First, as we have already argued in the previous section, there can be no reconciliation without repentance by the perpetrator. Without repentance, forgiveness cannot be effective in bringing about reconciliation. Secondly, since forgiveness is aimed at bringing about reconciliation, the one who forgives should also desire the repentance of the perpetrator and should therefore 'preach repentance to those who sin against us or against anyone else'. However, the Kairos document is wrong in claiming that repentance is a condition not only for reconciliation but also for forgiveness. It remains possible for the victim to forswear all resentment and to forgive even though this does not by itself suffice to bring about reconciliation. Thus the former anti-apartheid cleric Dr Frank Chikane declared that he wanted those who tried to assassinate him to repent, admit it and apologize. However, 'Chikane said he had forgiven his tormentors, but "until the perpetrator says 'I am sorry and want to change and live a different life,' he becomes a prisoner forever, even if I have forgiven him. So my forgiveness does not liberate the perpetrator".'[16] By forgiving, the victim is freed from the bonds of resentment and victimhood, but this does not free the perpetrator from being a prisoner of his or her old guilty self. Only repentance and a change of heart can do that.

We have argued above that forgiveness can only be freely given. If, however, repentance were a condition for forgiveness, this would deny the freedom of forgiveness in two ways. First the perpetrator could oblige the victim to forgive by repenting and thus fulfilling the condition. Secondly, by refusing to repent, the perpetrator could make it impossible for the victim to forgive and be released from the bonds of resentment. On this point Tutu argues that contrition on the part of the perpetrator

> is a very great help to the one who wants to forgive, but it is not absolutely indispensable … If the victim could forgive only when the culprit confesses, then the victim would be locked into the culprit's whim, locked into victimhood, whatever her own attitude or intention. This would be palpably unjust.[17]

It is clear that the price of reconciliation is difficult for us to pay. We are reluctant to forgive those who damage our interests and we are reluctant to repent when we damage the interests of others. Nevertheless, it is only through sincere repentance and

---

[15] *Challenge to the Church. A Theological Comment on the Political Crisis in South Africa*, publication of the Programme to Combat Racism of the World Council of Churches, November 1985.

[16] Quoted in the *Mail and Guardian* newspaper, 31 October 2000.

[17] Tutu, *No Future without Forgiveness*, 220.

forgiveness that we can be reconciled with each other and restorative justice can be done. So it is with reconciliation between us humans. Does this also apply to reconciliation with God?

Divine Forgiveness

In the previous chapter I argued that our ultimate happiness consists in enjoying loving fellowship with God. We enjoy such fellowship when God identifies with us by making our ultimate happiness his own concern, and we identify with God by making his will our own. As in the case of human fellowship, this mutual identification is necessarily free in the sense that one partner can neither compel nor oblige the other to reciprocate the fellowship. In this sense we cannot *compel* God to love us. God remains free in his love. Likewise, God cannot compel us to reciprocate his love for us since, then, our response would not be love or fellowship. Neither can we *oblige* God to identify with us by somehow earning his love through doing his will. God's love cannot be earned; not because the price is too high or our efforts too feeble, but because it is love, and by definition love cannot be earned but only bestowed freely. We simply cannot talk about love or fellowship in terms of rewards, which might or might not be merited. Thus we cannot earn ultimate happiness by doing God's will. Our salvation remains a gracious favour freely bestowed on us by God. On the other hand, God does not try to 'earn' our love by his offer of salvation. He wants us to love him because we identify with him, and not on account of what we can receive from him in return. If we love heaven rather than God, then our efforts are directed towards our own interests and we fail to identify with the will of God.

This is in fact precisely what we do. We disrupt the fellowship with God by trying to pursue our own finite interests rather than identifying with his will. In this way sin is not primarily a state of corruption calling for a divine manipulative cure, nor guilt to be wiped out through punishment or satisfaction, but estrangement from God requiring reconciliation. As in the case of damaged human fellowship, the necessary and sufficient conditions for reconciliation with God are not punishment or satisfaction or condonation, but repentance and forgiveness. If by penitence we repudiate the damage that through selfishness and unfaithfulness we have done to our fellowship with God, and through acts of penance we try to express our change of heart and the sincerity of this repudiation, and if God should grant us our desire for restoration of our fellowship by forgiving us, then we shall be reconciled with him and our fellowship will be restored. Nothing more than this is required. In the words of D.M. Baillie,

> God will freely forgive even the greatest sins, if only the sinners will repent and turn from their evil ways. Nothing else is needed, no expiation, no offerings, for God has everything already. Sincere repentance is enough, and a real turning from sin to God; and then the sinner can count on God's mercy.[18]

---

[18] D.M. Baillie, *God Was in Christ* (London, 1961), 176.

The justice of God is restorative rather than retributive. In Luke 23:39–43 we read about Jesus and the two criminals crucified with him:

> One of the criminals hanging there taunted him: 'Are you the Messiah? Save yourself and us.' But the other rebuked him: 'Have you no fear of God? You are under the same sentence as he is. In our case it is plain justice; we are paying the price for our misdeeds. But this man has done nothing wrong.' And he said, 'Jesus, remember me when you come to your throne.' Jesus answered, 'Truly I tell you: today you will be with me in Paradise.'

The 'plain justice' of the criminals on the cross was retributive, the kind of justice in which 'we are paying the price for our misdeeds'. This is the justice of Hell where we suffer eternal punishment for our sins. This is the kind of justice we tend to seek in relation to each other, the justice that fails to restore our broken fellowships. Jesus, however, sought the restorative justice of Paradise. This is the justice of God that restores us to the fellowship with him which is ultimate happiness.

In these respects reconciliation with God is like reconciliation with other people. Here, too, the necessary conditions for reconciliation are penitence and forgiveness. However, God is not like other people, and there are at least four important respects in which divine forgiveness differs from being forgiven by other people.[19] First, as we have pointed out above, your forgiveness depends on your free decision. Since I cannot cause your forgiveness, there are limits to the extent to which I could count on it. I am dependent on you to forgive. As we have shown, it is very difficult for us as humans to forgive and suppress our resentment for the injury others cause us. The price for forgiveness is high and we are very reluctant to pay it. For this reason we tend to seek retributive justice from those who injure us since this does not require us to forgive and upholds our right to receive satisfaction for what has been done to us. With God this is different. Because he is *perfect* in love, there is never the slightest likelihood that he will ever fail to forgive and be reconciled with those who are truly penitent. As we have said, the justice of God is restorative rather than retributive. It is the justice of I John 1:9: 'If we confess our sins, he is *just* and may be trusted to forgive our sins and cleanse us from every kind of wrong.' Unlike us, God is not reluctant to forgive. However, this is not because we somehow earn or necessitate his forgiveness by our penitence. On the contrary, Divine forgiveness remains a free gift. As Peter Baelz explains,

> the penitent is not only voicing his sincere grief and contrition when he asks for forgiveness; he is also asking for something which he has no moral right to expect. He is asking for a new, undeserved expression of the divine love which will restore him to a right relationship. Although in one sense he may be confident of the unchanging love of God, in another sense that is just what he has no *right* to presume upon. To presume upon love is to blaspheme against it: '*Dieu pardonnera, car c'est son métier.*'[20]

---

[19] I have also developed these points elsewhere. See my *What Are We Doing When We Pray?* (London, 1984), 82–5.

[20] P.R. Baelz, *Prayer and Providence* (New York, 1968), 107.

Although I could be infinitely more confident of divine forgiveness than of human forgiveness, both kinds of forgiveness remain equally free and unmerited.

Secondly, when I express my penitence to someone whom I have injured, I inform that person of the fact that I am penitent and desire forgiveness. Without my expression of penitence, the other cannot know that I am penitent and that his or her forgiveness would restore our broken fellowship. With God this is different, for God knows the secrets of my heart without my having to inform him. As Kierkegaard explains, 'the person making the confession is not ... like one that confides in a friend to whom sooner or later he reveals things that the friend did not previously know. The all-knowing One does not get to know something about the maker of the confession.'[21]

Although our expressions of penitence do not tell God something he does not already know, they do acknowledge and welcome the fact that he knows it:

> We confess in order to express our acceptance to this fact, our willingness to be so known, and our desire to enter as far as we can into this searching knowledge God has of us. We stop the life of concealment, of pretending that no one knows or needs know. We say we know we are living in the light, we are content to have it so, only more so, we want to be wholly in the light if possible.[22]

If divine forgiveness is to be effective in restoring the personal fellowship between God and the penitent, then this *acknowledgement* is a necessary condition for being reconciled with God. Without such acknowledgement the penitent remains an *object* of God's knowledge but does not become a *person* in relation to God. C.S. Lewis explains this point as follows:

> To be known by God is to be ... in the category of things. We are, like earthworms, cabbages and nebulae, objects of divine knowledge. But when we (a) become aware of the fact – the present fact, not the generalisation – and (b) assent with all our will to be so known, then we treat ourselves, in relation to God, not as things but as persons. We have unveiled. Not that any veil could have baffled his sight. The change is in us. The passive changes to the active. Instead of merely being known, we show, we tell, we offer ourselves to view ... By unveiling, by confessing our sins and 'making known' our requests, we assume the high rank of persons before him. And he, descending, becomes a Person to us.[23]

It is therefore not sufficient to say with Kierkegaard that 'not God, but you, the maker of the confession, get to know something by your act of confession'.[24] The maker of the confession does not merely get to *know* something. He also assumes the status of

[21] S. Kierkegaard, *Purity of Heart*, trans. D.V. Steere (New York, 1956), 50.

[22] J.N. Ward, *The Use of Praying* (London, 1967), 43.

[23] C.S. Lewis, *Letters to Malcolm: Chiefly on Prayer* (London, 1964), 33.

[24] Kierkegaard, *Purity of Heart*, 51. See also D.Z. Phillips, *The Concept of Prayer* (London, 1968), ch. 4.

a person and therefore of the sort of being with whom God can restore personal fellowship.

A third difference between divine and human forgiveness is the following. Since my asking *your* forgiveness is aimed at restoring the fellowship that I marred by injuring *you*, it only makes sense if I ask you to forgive what I did to you and not the injury I do to others or my moral transgressions in general. In fact, your forgiveness does not even cover the injury I do to you completely, for, as W.G. Maclagan points out, 'when ... injury is considered not as injury but in its character of wickedness or evil-doing we recognize that, so regarded, it is something that no man, not even the person injured, can properly be said to forgive. Men can forgive injuries; they cannot forgive sins'.[25] Thus you can forgive my injuring *your good*, but not the fact that in so doing I outrage *goodness* as such. At this point the parallel between divine and human forgiveness breaks down: unlike us, God can and does forgive sins. However, it does not break down completely, for, as I have argued in the previous chapter,[26] a believer is someone who accepts the will of God as the *ultimate* standard of goodness. It follows from this that all sin, as outrage against goodness, is for the believer an outrage against the will of God and, as such, an injury to God in which the loving fellowship with God is marred. For this reason I can ask divine forgiveness for *all* my sins, whereas I can only ask your forgiveness for injury I do to you.

This third difference between divine and human forgiveness entails a fourth. If I am penitent and you forgive me, my fellowship with you could be restored. But your forgiveness does not restore my fellowship with God that was also marred by the injury I did to you. For this reason, as I argued in the previous section, if I am a believer, I would not be satisfied with your forgiveness alone. I would want God's forgiveness as well. Only then would my sin be blotted out completely. Of God alone can it be said that 'as far as the east is from the west, so far does he remove our transgressions from us' (Psalm 103:12). Only if I know that God accepts me, can I come to accept myself. Or stronger: if I know that God accepts me, it would be meaningless for me *not* to accept myself. As D.Z. Phillips explains, 'it makes sense to say, "My friend forgives me, but I cannot forgive myself", but it makes no sense to say, "God forgives me, but I cannot forgive myself" ... Being able to see that one is forgiven by God entails being able to live with oneself.'[27]

In brief: through sincere penitence and divine forgiveness, our loving fellowship with God can be restored. Such fellowship bestows ultimate meaning on my very existence and enables me to 'live with myself'. According to the Christian tradition, this is ultimate happiness. In order to achieve this, however, more than divine forgiveness is required. Sincere repentance and a change of heart on our part are also necessary. How is such a change of heart to be achieved?

---

[25] W.G. Maclagan, *The Theological Frontier of Ethics* (London, 1961), 161.

[26] See also my *Speaking of a Personal God* (Cambridge, 1992), sections 4.3 and 4.4.

[27] Phillips, *The Concept of Prayer*, 63.

Change of Heart

I have argued that a relationship of loving fellowship can only be established, maintained and restored in mutual freedom. This means that both forgiveness and penitence should be free and cannot be caused or earned. A change of heart that is not freely chosen by the perpetrator cannot be authentic. It remains up to the perpetrator to decide whether he or she desires to be reconciled or to remain a prisoner of his or her old guilty self. This also applies to reconciliation with God. God cannot force us to be happy since he cannot force us to love him or to be reconciled with him. In the words of St Bernard: 'I would regain, said God to himself, the heart of this noble creature, man: but if I force him against his will, I shall have but a stubborn mule not a man, for he will not come to me of himself nor with good-will.'[28] On the other hand, there are a number of serious obstacles that prevent us from achieving such a change of heart. Even if we should freely decide to change our ways and to become reconciled with God, we are unable to do so by ourselves. Even though God cannot cause us to be reconciled with him, he can in various ways both urge and enable us to do so. In fact, God does not only desire us to be reconciled with him, but he also actively removes the obstacles that prevent us from achieving such reconciliation. The steps that are required to enable us to become penitent and achieve a change of heart, have traditionally been described in terms of the various stages of the *via mystica* along which mystics like St Bernard sought to find ultimate happiness in the love of God.

Denis divided the journey to God into three stages, referred to as *purification* (or purgation), *illumination* (or enlightenment) and *ecstasy* (or union).[29] In various forms, this threefold division can be found in the thought and experience of very many mystics and is therefore useful as a schema for describing their way to ultimate happiness through reconciliation with God. In the Protestant tradition, this schema is also reflected in the threefold division of the *Heidelberg Catechism* of 1563. In answer to the second question, the catechism states that it is necessary for me to know three things in order 'to live and die happily': 'First, the greatness of my sin and misery. Second, how I am redeemed from all my sin and misery. Third, how I am to be thankful to God for such redemption.' Let us examine these stages more closely. In doing so I will broadly follow the way these are explained by St Bernard.[30]

---

[28] Quoted by Etienne Gilson, *The Mystical Theology of St. Bernard* (London, 1940), 78.

[29] 'Threefold is the way to God. The first is the way of purification, in which the mind is inclined to learn true wisdom. The second is the way of illumination, in which the mind by contemplation is kindled to the burning of love. The third is the way of union, in which the mind by understanding, reason and spirit is led up by God alone.' This celebrated passage from Denis is quoted by Evelyn Underhill in *The Essentials of Mysticism and Other Essays* (London, 1920), 11.

[30] Bernard of Clairvaux explains the stages of the mystic way in his *Sermons on the Song of Songs*, 4 vols (Kalamazoo, MI, 1971–80) and in his treatise *On the Twelve Steps of Humility and Pride, and On Loving God* (London, 1985). See also his *Treatise on Grace and Free Will* (Kalamazoo, MI, 1988). For an excellent exposition of his mystical theology, see Gilson, *The Mystical Theology of St. Bernard.*

The first stage of the *via mystica* is that of *purification* in which we learn repentance, self-denial and humility. We must first take leave of what Bernard calls the *regio dissimilitudinis* (land of unlikeness)[31] before we can even start to change ourselves and regain the Divine likeness, which we have lost through sin. For the mystic this remodelling of character is the essential first step on the way to God: 'False ways of feeling and thinking, established complexes which have acquired for us an almost sacred character, and governed though we knew it not all our reactions to life – these must be broken up.'[32] In order to achieve this kind of purification, we must come to know ourselves for what we really are. In the words of the catechism, the first thing to know is 'the greatness of my sin and misery'. We should come to realize that we lack Socratic self-knowledge and are therefore fundamentally mistaken about the true nature of our daimon. In this way the prodigal son had first to admit that his search for ultimate happiness by craving finite riches and fame rather than in doing the will of his father, was bound to fail and should therefore be abandoned:

> Then he came to his senses: 'How many of my father's hired servants have more food than they can eat,' he said, 'and here am I, starving to death! I will go at once to my father, and say to him, "Father, I have sinned against God and against you; I am no longer fit to be called your son".' (Luke 15:17–19)

Repentance, self-denial and humility are difficult if not impossible for most of us. The trouble is that our estrangement from God has made us ignorant of him and of ourselves. Like the prodigal son in the distant country, we become quite unaware of the fact that we are mistaken about the nature of our true daimon. We fail to realize that our search for happiness in finite goods cannot make us ultimately happy. Self-denial becomes impossible for us when we are quite satisfied with ourselves as we are. Furthermore, in our estrangement we have not only lost our Socratic self-knowledge, but we have also become ignorant of God. For most of us it is by no means obvious that ultimate happiness can be found in the love of God. Seeking happiness in finite goods is both the only and the obvious thing to do. Not only do we not know God, we do not even know who God is. For this reason we have lost the ability to even desire reconciliation with God, let alone to seek it. We cannot seek a 'union of wills' with God, because we do not know what his will for us is. We cannot seek divine forgiveness for we do not know whether God is long-suffering enough to forgive.

> The tragedy of the human situation lies in the fact that sinful man has lost the knowledge of the God against whom he has sinned, and *this is the punishment* which sin can never escape. The sins of men have built their own prison, in which the windows are beyond the prisoners' reach: they have forgotten what the sunlight world of freedom was like. They *cannot* repent, because they do not know whom they have offended.[33]

---

[31] See Gilson, *The Mystical Theology of St. Bernard*, ch. 2.

[32] Underhill, *The Essentials of Mysticism*, 12.

[33] Burnaby, *Christian Words and Christian Meanings*, 94–5.

In order to be set free from this prison, our minds, in the words of Denis, must be 'inclined to learn true wisdom'. This happens when God makes us aware of our state of estrangement, and reveals himself to us as the one in whose love we can find ultimate happiness. In this way the first stage of the mystic way is aimed at achieving humility before God. In his third sermon on the Song of Songs, dealing with the verse 'let him kiss me with the kisses of his mouth' (Song of Songs 1:2), Bernard compares the three stages of the *via mystica* with three kisses. The first stage is called 'the kiss of the feet' with reference to Mary Magdalene kissing the feet of Jesus:

> It is up to you wretched sinner, to humble yourself as this happy penitent did so that you may be rid of your wretchedness. Prostrate yourself on the ground, take hold of his feet, soothe them with kisses, sprinkle them with your tears and so wash not them but yourself.[34]

The second stage in the *via mystica* is that in which we aspire to the 'union of wills' with God. Like the prodigal son, we desire to become like one of the servants who devote their days to doing the will of the father. How is this 'union of wills' to be achieved? According to Bernard, God has endowed us with freedom from necessity or freedom of choice (*liberum arbitrium*). However, on account of our estrangement from God this freedom has become impotent when it comes to doing his will. Thus we cannot achieve the 'union of wills' with God by merely choosing to make God's will our own and living our lives accordingly. In order to do this, we need to regain two other freedoms that we have lost on account of the fall: the freedom from sin or freedom of counsel (*liberum consilium*) and the freedom from misery or freedom of pleasure (*liberum complacitum*).[35]

In his *Treatise on Grace and Free Choice* Bernard equates these three freedoms with the image and likeness of God in us: 'I believe that in these three freedoms there is contained the image and likeness of the Creator in which we were made; that in freedom of choice lies the image, and in the other two is contained a certain twofold likeness.'[36] In other words, we are created in the image of God in the sense that we are free and responsible personal agents endowed with the ability to make choices rather than mere animals or inanimate objects who are determined by (internal and external) necessity. Through the fall we are deprived of our likeness to God (that is, our freedom from sin and from suffering), but not of the image of God (that is, our freedom from necessity). We remain free and responsible personal agents even when subject to sin and suffering. And it is not as objects driven by necessity, but as free and responsible personal agents that God in his grace wants to restore our loving fellowship with him and thus save us from sin and suffering. To this purpose he gives

---

[34] Bernard, *Song of Songs*, sermon 3.

[35] On Bernard's distinction between these three freedoms and the way in which this distinction is also defended by John Calvin, see my paper on 'Calvin, Bernard and the freedom of the will', *Religious Studies* 30 (1994), 437–55.

[36] Bernard, *Treatise on Grace and Free Will*, 9.28.

us again the two freedoms that we have lost. In other words, the *liberum arbitrium* is a necessary but not a sufficient condition for restoring our relationship of love with God: without the exercise of free choice we cannot be saved; by itself it is impotent and cannot achieve salvation. We can only regain our relationship with God if by grace God restores to us the freedom from sin and the freedom from suffering. According to Bernard, these two freedoms are restored to us respectively in the second and third stages of the *via mystica*. What do these two freedoms entail, and why does our *liberum arbitrium* fail to achieve ultimate happiness without them?

First, even if we should freely decide to make God's will our own and live our lives in accordance with it, we cannot carry out this decision unless we know what the will of God is. This is the first reason for the impotence of our *liberum arbitrium*: we cannot do God's will because we do not know what it is. It is here that we are in need of the gift of enlightenment.

> If you do not know what he wills with whom you have reached agreement of will, shall he not say of you that you have a zeal for God, but it is not knowledgeable? And if you think this unimportant, remember that it is written, 'he that does not know will not be known' (I Corinthians 14:38) … My advice is that you go now to the Word, and he will teach you his ways, so that you will not go astray in your journey and, desiring the good but not recognizing it, wander in a pathless place instead of along the highway.[37]

But enlightenment is not enough. Even if we were to know what God's will is and freely choose to live our lives in accordance with it, this does not mean that we have the ability or the strength to do so. In order to live according to the will of God, I will have to overcome not only the devil and the world but above all myself: 'If you attempt it in your own strength, it will be as though you were trying to stop the raging of a torrent, or to make the Jordan run backwards.'[38] This is the second reason for the impotence of our *liberum arbitrium*: 'To will lies in our power indeed as a result of free choice, but not to carry out what we will.'[39] Here we need the gift of strength or empowerment:

> Know how hard the climb is, and how the attempt is doomed to failure without the help of the Word … Nothing shows more clearly the almighty power of the Word than that he makes all-powerful all those who put their hope in him. For 'all things are possible to one who believes' (Mark 9:23). If all things are possible to him, he must be all-powerful. Thus if the mind does not rely upon itself, but is strengthened by the Word, it can gain such command over itself that no unrighteousness will have power over it.[40]

If in this way we have been enlightened to know God's will and empowered to do God's will, then 'we might also, by counsel, choose the licit as more suitable and

[37] Bernard, *Song of Songs*, sermon 85.
[38] Bernard, *Song of Songs*, sermon 85.
[39] Bernard, *Treatise on Grace and Free Will*, 6.16.
[40] Bernard, *Song of Songs*, sermon 85.

reject the illicit as harmful. Then we would not only be free in our choice, but undoubtedly also free in counsel, and consequently free from sin.'[41]

In the second stage of the *via mystica*, therefore, we are freed from sin by the gifts of enlightenment to know God's will and empowerment to do God's will. In this way we are freed from the limitations of our knowledge and capacities and thus enabled to aspire to the union of wills, which is the love of God. While Bernard calls the first stage the kiss of the feet, he describes the second as that of being lifted up to kiss the hand of Christ:

> First it must cleanse your stains, then it must raise you up. How raise you? By giving you the grace to dare to aspire. You wonder what this may be. I see it as the grace of the beauty of temperance and the fruits that befit repentance, the works of the religious man. These are the instruments that will lift you from the dunghill and cause your hopes to soar. On receiving such a grace then, you must kiss his hand, that is, you must give glory to his name, not to yourself.[42]

The *liberum consilium* restored in the second stage, is therefore the freedom from sin that enables the righteous to know God's will and to act in accordance with it. This freedom enables us to live a life of virtue, but it does not guarantee that this is always easy or pleasant for us, and therefore it does not free us from suffering:

> It is one thing to be controlled in virtue, and another to be delighted by sweetness ... It is an honour, therefore, to stand firm, to resist, to meet force with force – these are considered works of virtue – but it is hard work. For defending your honour with toil is not the same as possessing it in peace. Nor is being moved by virtue the same as enjoying virtue.[43]

Ultimate happiness does not consist in being virtuous from a sense of obligation, but in doing God's will out of love. This is only possible when out of love God's will has become our own. This is the experience of union of wills which is only granted to us in the third stage of the *via mystica*. Only when God's will has become our own, do we regain not only our freedom from sin (*liberum consilium*) but also our freedom from misery (*liberum complacitum*). For this it is not enough that we receive the gifts of enlightenment and empowerment. According to St Bernard we also need the gift of 'wisdom' or 'taste':

> Where there is love, there is no toil, but a taste. Perhaps *sapientia*, that is wisdom, is derived from *sapor*, that is taste, because, when it is added to virtue, like some seasoning, it adds taste to something which by itself is tasteless and bitter. I think it would be permissible to define wisdom as a taste for goodness. We lost this taste almost from the creation of our human race. How many good actions are performed without the doers having any taste for them, because they are compelled to do them by their way of life or by some circumstance or necessity?

---

[41] Bernard, *Treatise on Grace and Free Will*, 4.11.
[42] *Song of Songs*, sermon 3.
[43] Bernard, *Song of Songs*, sermon 85.

> ... But those who ... are wise ... delight in goodness because they have a taste for
> it ... Happy is the mind that is protected by a taste for good and a hatred of evil,
> for this is what it means to be reformed to wisdom, and to know by experience
> and to rejoice in the victory of wisdom ... It looks to virtue to sustain tribulations
> with fortitude, and to wisdom to rejoice in those tribulations. To strengthen your
> heart and to wait upon the Lord – that is virtue; to taste and to see that the Lord is
> good – that is wisdom.[44]

Through the gift of wisdom or taste granted us in the final stage of the mystic way,
God's will in fact becomes our own and we are able to enjoy the ecstatic experience of
loving union with God. While the second stage is characterized by *ardent love* in the
sense of an ardent desire for union with God, that is 'the hope of higher things', the third
is characterized by *pure love* as the ecstatic enjoyment of this union. The ardent love of
the second stage makes us bold enough to approach him with candour and thus casts out
fear. The pure love of the third casts out desire as well. Here there is no need for desire
since there is perfect possession. Bernard characterizes this as 'the kiss of the lips':

> Once you have had this twofold experience of God's benevolence in these two
> kisses, you need no longer feel abashed in aspiring to a holier intimacy. Growth in
> grace brings expansion of confidence. You will love with greater ardor, and knock
> on the door with greater assurance, in order to gain what you perceive to be still
> wanting in you. 'The one who knocks will always have the door opened to him'
> (Luke 11:10). It is my belief that to a person so disposed, God will not refuse that
> most intimate kiss of all, a mystery of supreme generosity and ineffable
> sweetness. You have seen the way that we must follow, in order of procedure:
> first, we cast ourselves at his feet, we weep before the Lord who made us,
> deploring the evil that we have done. Then we reach out to the hand that will lift
> us up, that will steady our trembling knees. And finally, when we shall have
> obtained these favors through many prayers and tears, we humbly dare to raise
> our eyes to his mouth, so divinely beautiful, not merely to gaze upon it, but – I say
> this with fear and trembling – to receive its kiss.[45]

This third stage differs in an important respect from the other two: the soul has no part
to play in achieving it. In the first two stages, according to Bernard, the soul is *led up*
to humility and to charity. Someone who is led, moves by himself and co-operates
with the one who leads. We therefore have to exert ourselves to acquire humility and
charity under the guidance of God. The third stage, however, is like the third heaven
to which St Paul refers in 2 Corinthians 12:2, since something more than leading is
required in order to reach it. Here the soul must be carried away or *caught up* (raptus)
by God. This stage is therefore literally an experience of *rapture* granted gratuitously
by God.[46] Thus, although the prodigal son aspired only to become a servant doing the
will of his father and considered himself unfit to be called a son, his father 'ran to
meet him, flung his arms around him and kissed him' (Luke 15:20).

---

[44] Bernard, *Song of Songs*, sermon 85.
[45] Bernard, *Song of Songs*, sermon 3.
[46] On this point see Gilson, *The Mystical Theology of St. Bernard*, 106.

Bernard admits that, in an absolute sense, this ecstatic union with God is only possible in the next life when we are freed from the limitations of our finite mortal existence:

> This vision is not for the present life; it is reserved for the next ... Neither sage nor saint nor prophet can or could ever see him as he is, while still in this mortal body; but whoever is found worthy will be able to do so when the body becomes immortal.[47]

Freedom from suffering (*liberum complacitum*) is only restored to us fully in the life of glory. Thus Bernard argues that 'there are three forms of freedom, as they have occurred to us: freedom from sin, from sorrow and from necessity. The last belongs to our natural condition; to the first we are restored by grace; and the second is reserved for us in our homeland'.[48]

This implies that *ultimate* happiness in the love of God cannot be attained in our mortal human state of finitude. This is not because God's loving identification with us is somehow flawed but because our human identification with the will of God remains finite and fallible. Although believers may find happiness in striving to realize the will of God in their lives, the finite nature of their identification with it causes God's will to retain for them the character of a law to which they should conform rather than becoming internalized as their own will. For this reason happiness remains finite and ambiguous in this life. This ambiguity is well expressed in the words of Psalm 119:1–5:

> Happy are they whose way of life is blameless,
> who conform to the law of the LORD.
> Happy are they who obey his instructions,
> who set their hearts on finding him;
> who have done no wrong,
> but have lived according to his will.
> You, Lord, have laid down your precepts
> that are to be kept faithfully.
> If only I might hold a steady course,
> keeping your statutes.

On the one hand, the righteous are happy when they 'have lived according to God's will', while on the other hand, God's will remains for them the 'law of the LORD' to which they are required to conform – 'precepts that are to be kept faithfully'. But then

---

[47] Bernard, *Song of Songs*, sermon 31.

[48] Bernard, *Treatise on Grace and Free Will*, 3.7. Similarly, Bernard argues that 'the first freedom, therefore, might be termed freedom of nature, the second of grace, the third of life or glory. For in the first place, we are created with free will and willing freedom, a creature noble in God's eyes. Secondly, we are reformed in innocence, a new creature in Christ; and thirdly, we are raised in glory, a perfect creature in the Spirit' (*Treatise on Grace and Free Will*, 7.7).

the righteous are not motivated by that perfect love in which God's will has become their own, but at most by gratitude to God for their redemption from sin. In the words of the *Heidelberg Catechism* (question 86): 'that with our whole life we may show ourselves thankful to God for his blessings, and that he may be glorified through us'. But then doing the will of God is fulfilling a debt of gratitude that we owe to God, rather than following Augustine's precept to 'love and do what you will'.[49] The experience of such a union of wills with God remains beyond us in this life. At most, Bernard suggests, some mystics may sometimes enjoy the grace of experiencing what might be called brief glimpses of eternity. These moments of ecstasy are rare and of brief duration.[50] In spite of the intensity of mystic love, its transitory character makes the perfect union with the will of God incomplete in this life. In this life, therefore, the perfect love of God that is ultimate happiness remains for us an ideal to which we may ardently aspire rather than a present reality that we might enjoy.

The Matrix of Faith

Let me recapitulate. In this and the previous chapter I have been arguing that, for the believer, ultimate happiness consists in enjoying the loving fellowship of God. In such fellowship, God makes our ultimate happiness his very own concern, and we identify with God by making his will our own and living our lives joyfully in accordance with it. Because of our finitude and fallibility, however, we are unable to maintain this loving identification with God consistently, if at all. We therefore become estranged from God and can only regain ultimate happiness by being reconciled with him. The necessary and sufficient conditions for such reconciliation are divine forgiveness and, on our part, repentance and a change of heart by which we can again identify with God's will and live our lives joyfully in accordance with it. In order to achieve such a change of heart, we need first to realize that we can never be ultimately happy in our state of estrangement from God. Secondly, we need that God should *enlighten* our minds to know his will for us, *empower* our wills that we may become able consistently to do his will and *inspire* our hearts that we may seek his will joyfully out of love and not merely out of duty.

I suggest that this could be understood as the basic structure or matrix of the faith by which Christians claim to attain ultimate happiness. However, I believe that this matrix as it has been explained in this and the previous chapter, could also be defended within the context of the Jewish and Islamic traditions. Although these three traditions within the faith of Abraham share this matrix, they differ in the metaphors, narratives and doctrines in terms of which they develop and explain it further. The doctrines of Atonement, Christology and the Trinity that I discuss in the next three chapters could therefore be understood as the specific forms in which the matrix of

---

[49] Augustine, *Homily on the First Epistle of St. John*, 7.8.
[50] Bernard, *Song of Songs*, sermon 32.

faith has been explained and developed within the Christian tradition. Thus understood, these doctrines cease to be mere theological constructions or theories but have their meaning and function within the existential context of the believer's search for ultimate happiness.

PART 3
CHRISTIAN DOCTRINE:
INTERPRETING THE MATRIX

CHAPTER 4

The Doctrine of Atonement

A Point of Departure

In Chapter 1 I argued that religious beliefs are always existential in the sense that they are directly connected with the ways in which we relate to God, in the actions and attitudes in which we respond to God and to the ways in which God relates to us. In this way our spirituality and the life of fellowship with God provide the necessary existential context within which Christian doctrines are to be understood. When doctrines are disconnected from this context, it becomes unclear what existential relevance they have for our lives. Such doctrines strike us as mere theoretical constructions produced by academic theologians. They may be of intellectual interest to such theologians, but are of little interest to ordinary believers. This is one of the reasons why ordinary believers today have great difficulty in making sense of the classical doctrines of Christology and the Trinity. In the words of Maurice Wiles:

> the modern reader who turns, without knowledge of their historical context, to the Athanasian Creed or the Chalcedonian Definition is likely to jump to the conclusion that their authors must have been academic theologians, whose concern was the construction of detailed schemes of intellectual orthodoxy bearing only the most remote relation to the realities of the spiritual life.[1]

These considerations provide an important clue to the order in which theologians should deal with the various key doctrines of the Christian tradition. Theologians should start off by reflecting on the nature of the spiritual life as the way along which believers seek to attain ultimate happiness. In the previous two chapters I have thus tried to reflect on what I take to be the necessary point of departure for understanding Christian doctrine. This leads naturally to a consideration of the doctrine of atonement taken as an explanation of the way in which we can be reconciled with God and thus be liberated from our bondage to sin, estrangement and unhappiness:

> The English word 'atonement' is derived from the words 'at-one-ment', to make two parties at one, to reconcile two parties one to another. It means essentially reconciliation ... In current usage, the phrase 'to atone for' means the undertaking of a course of action designed to undo the consequences of a wrong act with a view to the restoration of the relationship broken by the wrong act.[2]

---

[1] Maurice Wiles, *The Christian Fathers* (London, 1977), 83.

[2] James Atkinson, 'Atonement', in Alan Richardson (ed.), *A Dictionary of Christian Theology* (London, 1969), 18. See also John Burnaby, *Christian Words and Christian Meanings* (London, 1955), 95–6.

Only when we have achieved some clarity on these questions, can we proceed to a consideration of the issues of Christology: what role does Jesus play in the Atonement and in what sense does this entail the claim that he is both human and divine? After that we will be in the position to consider the doctrine of the Trinity: what role do the Father and the Holy Spirit have to fulfil in overcoming our estrangement and what does this entail for the way in which we are to understand the triune nature of God? This, in brief, is the programme for the chapters that follow. In this chapter I consider the ways in which the doctrine of atonement has usually been understood in the Christian tradition. The next chapter is devoted to the issues of Christology and Chapter 6 to the doctrine on the Trinity.

Strangely enough, the historical development of Christian doctrine proceeded in the reverse order from the one proposed here. The earliest controversies among the Church Fathers dealt with the divinity of Christ and the Spirit and culminated in the Trinitarian doctrine of Constantinople (381). After that the Fathers of the Church turned their attention to the dual nature of Christ and reached a settlement on this at Chalcedon (451). In all this the doctrine of the Atonement was hardly an issue of debate. In the words of J.N.D. Kelly,

> the student who seeks to understand the soteriology of the fourth and early fifth centuries will be sharply disappointed if he expects to find anything corresponding to the elaborately worked out syntheses which the contemporary theology of the Trinity and the Incarnation presents. In both these latter departments controversy forced fairly exact definition on the Church, whereas the redemption did not become a battle-ground for rival schools until the twelfth century.[3]

Although the Church Fathers entertained various ideas on the nature of salvation, these were never a topic of credal definition. The Nicene Creed merely states that the incarnation was 'for us men and for our salvation' but what this means was never precisely defined. According to Wiles, this is something for which we should be grateful: 'Man's need and its remedy is too varied a thing to lend itself satisfactorily to such systematized treatment ... The teaching of the Fathers on this theme has its faults, but its unsystematic character and its many-sidedness are not to be classed among them.'[4] John Burnaby explains this lack of definition by pointing out that the Fathers had 'many theories of the meaning and method of the Atonement, but none of them had been found so defective or misleading as to evoke from the Church a formal statement of "orthodox" doctrine'.[5]

In spite of their lack of systematic reflection and unified vision on the nature of salvation, the Father's views on this did play an important part as the background to which they appealed in their debates on Christology and the Trinity. In a way therefore their unsystematic ideas on the salvation did precede their doctrinal

---

[3] J.N.D. Kelly, *Early Christian Doctrines* (London, 1977), 375.

[4] Wiles, *The Christian Fathers*, 107.

[5] John Burnaby, *The Belief of Christendom. A Commenary on the Nicene Creed* (London, 1959), 115.

definitions on Christology and the Trinity. According to Wiles they 'were passionately concerned to lay hold of and propagate the gospel of salvation. This was their dominant concern, it was this that drove them on step by step in their task of doctrinal definition'.[6] If this was their dominant concern, as Wiles argues, we should ask how they understood this gospel of salvation. What was the nature of the human need for salvation and what did the coming of Christ do to meet this need?

Patristic Ideas on Atonement

The Fathers held 'a variety of theories [on the nature of salvation], to all appearance unrelated and even mutually incompatible, existing side by side and sometimes sponsored by the same theologian'.[7] According to Kelly, three of these are particularly significant.[8] We could refer to them as the theories of recapitulation, ransom and sacrifice.

The recapitulation theory was based on the Platonist assumptions entertained by the Fathers. First, it assumed that salvation entailed a form of 'divinization': being saved means being 'made partakers in the divine nature' (2 Peter 1:4). Such salvation through divinization was brought about by the incarnation of Christ: 'Because of his immeasurable love he became what we are, that we might be what he is' (Irenaeus): 'He entered into humanity that we might be made divine' (Athanasius). Atonement in the sense of 'at-one-ment' was therefore not understood as personal reconciliation restoring what Bernard calls the 'union of love' with God, but rather as being taken up into the unity of the Divine. This view of salvation is analogous to that of the unitive mystics in the Middle Ages. Secondly, the incarnation of Christ was understood here in terms of the Platonic assumption that the universal is more real than the particular. Thus humanity as a whole was viewed as a single universal entity that was more real than particular human beings. Accordingly, the incarnation was not thought of primarily in terms of Christ becoming a particular human being, but rather of Christ assuming or summing up ('recapitulating') in himself humanity as a whole and thus divinizing humanity as a single universal entity. In this way Christ's humanity was conceived of in corporate terms.[9] The Pauline distinction between the first and the second Adam was also understood in these terms. Just as the whole of humanity fell into sin through the disobedience of the first Adam conceived of as a single corporate personality, the whole of humanity was divinized by being included in the corporate personality of Christ as the second Adam. By such divinization in Christ, humanity as a whole is saved from human mortality and from the consequences of the sin of the first Adam. Those of us who are not familiar with the Platonist assumptions of

---

[6] Wiles, *The Christian Fathers*, 83. See also Maurice Wiles, *The Making of Christian Doctrine* (Cambridge, 1967), ch. 5.

[7] Kelly, *Early Christian Doctrines*, 375.

[8] See also Maurice Wiles, *The Remaking of Christian Doctrine* (London, 1974), 64.

[9] See Wiles, *The Making of Christian Doctrine*, 109.

patristic thought, have great difficulty in making sense of this view of the Atonement. In the words of Maurice Wiles, 'the language in which the Fathers spoke of that salvation is language that falls strangely on our ears'.[10]

While the recapitulation theory takes the incarnation as such to be the means of salvation, the other two patristic views focus on the death of Christ and its meaning for our salvation. The rationale for the ransom theory can be explained as follows.[11] In general the Fathers regarded the Atonement not as something done *to* God but rather as something done *by* God. The question then arises: to what or to whom is the act of atonement directed if it is not directed to God? The usual answer was that atonement was an act of God directed against Satan. This was the obvious answer at a time when people were very much aware of the real hold that personalized powers of evil had on all departments of human life. The powers of sin and death were the personalized powers of Satan over human existence. The ransom theory develops a speculative mythology explaining God's victory over Satan in which humanity was freed from Satan's power. J.N.D. Kelly describes Gregory of Nyssa's version of this mythology as follows:

> It was through his own free choice that man fell into the Devil's clutches. The Devil, therefore, had a right to adequate compensation if he were to surrender him, and for God to have exercised *force majeure* would have been unfair and tyrannical. So he offered him the man Jesus as a ransom. When Satan saw him, born as he was of a virgin and renowned as he was as worker of miracles, he decided that the exchange was to his advantage. What he failed to realize was that the outward covering of human flesh concealed the immortal Godhead. Hence, when he accepted Jesus in exchange for mankind, he could not hold him; he was outwitted and caught, as a fish is by the bait which conceals the hook. There was no injustice in this, Gregory tried to show, for the Devil was only getting his deserts, and in any case God's action was going to contribute to his own ultimate benefit (Gregory shared the doctrine of his master, Origen, that in the final restoration the pains of the damned, Satan included, would come to an end).[12]

From our perspective today such speculative mythology must sound strange indeed. We can therefore sympathize with those of the Fathers, like Gregory of Nazianzus, who rejected the whole idea of God paying a ransom to Satan as blasphemous. Nevertheless, the ransom theory did have wide support among the Fathers because it enshrined two important intuitions that were fundamental to patristic thinking. First, the belief that evil was an objective personalized power which held humanity in its sway and, secondly, the conviction that God alone was able to save us from the power of evil. As human beings we are totally unable to free ourselves from this bondage. In our age, however, these intuitions are contrary to the conviction that human evil actions are not merely the effects but also the source of evil in the world and also that God's saving action does in some way or other involve human actions. God acts *in* the

---

[10] Wiles, *The Christian Fathers*, 91.

[11] See Wiles, *The Christian Fathers*, 99–103.

[12] Kelly, *Early Christian Doctrines*, 382.

things we do.[13] To deny this would deny all human responsibility both for the existence of evil and for the opposition to evil in the world. In the words of Sally McFague:

> In an era when evil powers were understood to be palpable principalities in contest with God for control of human beings and the cosmos, the metaphor of Christ as the victorious king and lord, crushing the evil spirits and thereby freeing the world from their control, was indeed a powerful one. In our situation, however, to envision evil as separate from human beings rather than as the outcome of human decisions and actions, and to see the solution of evil as totally a divine responsibility, would be not only irrelevant to our time and its needs but harmful to them, for that would run counter to one of the central insights of the new sensibility: the need for human responsibility in a nuclear age.[14]

Many of the Fathers also viewed Christ's death as a substitutionary sacrifice by which the just demands of God's law are fulfilled in our stead. Here human responsibility for evil is fully recognized. Since all humanity is part of the corporate personality of the first Adam, all human beings share in Adam's guilt. Salvation therefore entails being relieved of this corporate guilt and this is done through the fact that Christ paid the price on behalf of all humanity on the cross. Wiles points out that such pictures suggest an understanding of the Atonement as an act directed to God rather than an act initiated by God. For this reason the Fathers who developed this kind of picture tried to do so in ways that somehow still make God the agent of salvation. 'If it is God's law that has to be met, it is also God who meets it. If it is God who has to be reconciled, it is God also who is the reconciler.'[15] The Fathers never work out the idea of substitutionary sacrifice as a detailed theory as this was done in the twelfth century by St Anselm. I will discuss this view on the Atonement below.

It is clear that the Fathers did not develop any systematic theory on the atonement. The views described above should rather be taken as alternative metaphors that the Fathers use to indicate the meaning of the atonement without any attempt to develop them systematically or to integrate them in a coherent whole. The result is what Wiles calls 'a curious mixture of profound insights and preposterous theorizing'.[16] In the next chapter I will discuss the ways in which these views on the atonement provided a rationale for the patristic views in Christology.

The Universal and the Particular

All these patristic views on the Atonement entail the Platonic assumption that the universal is more real than the particular. From this perspective the fall of Adam is

---

[13] See chapter 5 of my *Speaking of a Personal God* (Cambridge, 1992).

[14] S. McFague, *Models of God* (London, 1987), 29–30

[15] Wiles, *The Christian Fathers*, 103.

[16] Wiles, *The Christian Fathers*, 107.

understood as a corporate act involving humanity as a whole. The result was that humanity as a whole was under the bondage of Satan, sin and death. Similarly humanity as a whole is taken to be the universal object of salvation. Humanity as a whole is 'recapitulated' in the corporate personality of Christ. The death of Christ is a ransom or a sacrifice on behalf of humanity as a whole. But how does this affect us as individual human beings? How is the corporate sin of Adam and the corporate salvation in Christ transmitted to individual human beings?

The general view was that through Adam all humanity had contracted the malady of sin. Sin is a state of corruption resulting from Adam's fall and was transmitted to all generations and thus to all individuals who are descended from Adam. All human beings have the disease and sooner or later it will show in the sins of their own wilful choosing. The Fathers held various views on the way in which the malady of sin is transmitted, but they were all agreed that sin is a universal state as a result of which all human beings participate in the state of sin and are responsible for their sinning.

It is here that Augustine developed the view that sin is concupiscence: the desire for finite pleasure instead of the love of God. This was basically the sin of Adam. One of the most potent forms of such finite pleasure is the excitement of sexual intercourse. Since sexual intercourse lies at the origin of every human being, all are born through sin and in this way inherit the state of corruption. But this state of corruption is also a state of guilt. Augustine appealed to the Latin version of Romans 5:12 where Paul refers to Adam 'in whom all have sinned'. For Augustine this means that all human beings were present in the voluntary agency of Adam as he freely willed his sinful act. All humans therefore share Adam's guilt and are under the just sentence of death and damnation.

There is, therefore, something universal and automatic about the way in which the state of corruption and guilt of humanity as a whole was transmitted to every individual human being. However, there was general agreement among the Fathers that no such automatism applied in the case of salvation. Only at the level of bare mortality did they consider the effects of Christ's incarnation and the resurrection to be automatic. Sinners and saints alike will participate in the resurrection. But with salvation from sin and receiving eternal blessing, such universal automatism does not apply. Here there is need for an explicit and chosen response on the part of the individual human being. Through the saving action of Christ the way is open for everyone to be saved. But each of us still has to choose to proceed along that way. The response of faith is our responsibility. It might be a very small contribution, but each individual human being who is to participate in the salvation in Christ must provide it. After all, if everything were the work of God in which we have no part to play, we could not explain why not everybody is in the state of faith and salvation. Since the state of corruption does not eliminate human free choice altogether, every individual human being is required to respond freely to the offer of salvation. Without this free response, salvation cannot be attained.

This was the general view held by the Fathers. Initially Augustine was also prepared to accept it. God can enable us in various ways to respond to his offer of salvation, but he cannot bring about our response as such without it ceasing to be ours.[17] Towards the end of his life, however, Augustine came to doubt whether this does adequate justice to the absolute priority of divine grace. If the consent of faith is necessary for salvation, and if we are able to provide this ourselves, then we can claim a part, even if only a small part, of the credit for our own salvation. Then all the credit will not go to the grace of God alone. Hence Augustine concluded that even the response of faith is brought about by God and not by us. Even our willing is brought about apart from us. This raises a problem: if God causes even the response of faith as such, how do we explain the fact that not everybody responds in faith? To this Augustine replied with the claim that God chose some to be recipients of his grace and others not. In the end it is the inscrutable will of God that decides who is to be saved and who is to suffer eternal damnation. Not all of humanity is included in the corporate personality of Christ. One part of humanity is and another part of it is not. Whereas participation of humanity in the fall of Adam is both automatic and universal, the 'recapitulation' of humanity in Christ is automatic but not universal.

In the sixteenth century John Calvin developed his doctrine of double predestination in which the divine determinism of the later Augustine was pushed to its logical conclusions. Not only the descendants of Adam but Adam himself was subject to divine determinism and therefore not a free agent in relation to God. Thus, even the fall itself was the result of an eternal divine decree. The human partner in the divine–human relation can at no time be other than a passive object of divine agency. From the very beginning God alone is an agent in his relationship to human beings. Thus, in his most uncompromisingly supralapsaristic moments[18] Calvin could argue that

> before the first man was created, God in his eternal counsel had determined what he willed to be done with the whole human race. In the hidden counsel of God it was determined that Adam should fall from the unimpaired condition of his nature, and by his defection should involve all his posterity in sentence of eternal death. Upon the same decree depends the distinction between elect and reprobate: as he adopted some for himself for salvation, he destined others for eternal ruin. While the reprobate are the vessels of the just wrath of God, and the elect vessels of his compassion, the ground of the distinction is to be sought in the pure will of God alone, which is the supreme rule of justice.[19]

The theological advantage of this view is that it radically excluded every ground for humans to claim credit for their own salvation: 'for it is by his grace you are saved, through trusting him; it is not your own doing. It is God's gift, not a reward for work

---

[17] See Augustine's treatise on *De Spiritu et Littera*, ch. 54. On this point see also chapter 3 of my *Speaking of a Personal God*.

[18] Calvin did not consistently maintain such divine determinism. Sometimes he seems to have allowed for free human agency in relation to God. Like Augustine he seems at times to have been in two minds on the issue. See my paper on 'Calvin, Bernard and the freedom of the will', *Religious Studies*, 30 (1994).

[19] John Calvin, 'Articles concerning predestination', in J.K.S. Reid (ed.), *Calvin: Theological Treatises* (Philadelphia, PA, 1956), 179.

done. There is nothing for anyone to boast of' (Ephesians 2:8–9). The claim that God alone can save was central to the thinking of the Fathers. The divine determinism of Augustine and Calvin was intended to make this principle absolutely safe. If human beings cannot be agents in relation to God, they can in no way be the agents of meritorious acts before God. Thus human salvation is radically by grace alone, and can in no way or part be earned or merited by human actions. All credit belongs to God alone. *Soli Deo gloria!*

However, the conceptual price to be paid for this advantage is rather high. First, such divine determinism accounts for the divine–human relationship in manipulative rather than in personal terms. Sin is not viewed as estrangement requiring personal reconciliation or 'at-one-ment'. It is seen, rather, as a state of corruption requiring a manipulative cure that God alone can provide. God's agency is the necessary and sufficient condition for human salvation. The human partner in this relationship becomes (in Strawson's phrase quoted above in Chapter 2) a passive object 'to be managed or handled or cured or trained' by God, who is the only active partner in the relationship. It is clear that this manipulative model cannot account for the spirituality of loving fellowship with God, as we described it in previous chapters. Strictly speaking, this view is a theory of *salvation* explaining how we can be freed from our state of corruption but not a theory of *atonement* explaining how we can be reconciled with God in our lives.

Secondly, if human beings are not agents in relation to God, they cannot perform meritorious acts, but neither can they perform acts that make them guilty before God. If we are merely objects of divine manipulation, we can in no way be held responsible for the way we behave or for the state of corruption in which we find ourselves. Human beings cannot claim any credit for being saved from their state of corruption. But neither can they be blamed for being in it in the first place.

Thirdly, if God is the only agent in the relation, he is not only responsible for our salvation, but also for our state of corruption. Both the salvation (of some) and the eternal ruin (of others) result from God's 'eternal councel', which also 'determined that Adam should fall from the unimpaired condition of his nature, and by his defection should involve all his posterity in sentence of eternal death'! Then God is not only the origin of all good but also the author of all evil. It is logically incoherent to claim, as Calvin does in the 'Articles concerning predestination', that 'while the will of God is the supreme and primary cause of all things, and God holds the devil and the godless subject to his will, nevertheless God cannot be called the cause of sin, nor the author of evil, nor subject to any guilt.'

Fourthly, on this model it becomes rather difficult to explain how the incarnation or the death of Christ on Calvary was *necessary* for our salvation. Our salvation results from God's 'eternal councel' rather than from the merit of Christ. The latter is at most a contingently chosen means for effecting the former, but in no way logically necessary. It would be quite conceivable for an omnipotent God to cancel our state of corruption by an exercise of his infinite power alone. Thus, in the articles quoted above, Calvin declares explicitly that 'while we are elected in Christ, nevertheless that God reckons us among his own is prior in order to his making us members of Christ'. But then the question arises as to what the merit of Christ adds to the *prior* fact that 'God reckons us among his own'. A similar question can be raised with reference to the following statement by Calvin:

> When we treat of the merit of Christ, we do not place the beginning in him, but ascend to the ordination of God as the primary cause, because of his mere good pleasure he appointed a Mediator to purchase salvation for us ... There is nothing to prevent the justification of man from being the gratuitous result of the mere mercy of God, and, at the same time, to prevent the merit of Christ from intervening in subordination to this mercy.[20]

If the 'mere mercy of God' is sufficient, it is hard to see why the 'intervention of the merit of Christ' is necessary for the 'purchase of salvation for us'.

Penal Substitution

These difficulties arise when the divine–human relation is viewed in manipulative terms. They could be avoided by interpreting it in terms of an *agreement of rights and obligations* such as I described in the previous chapter. In this relationship each partner is a personal agent who accepts certain obligations towards the other and can be held responsible for fulfilling these obligations. In the Jewish and Christian traditions the covenant relationship between God and human persons has often been interpreted on the analogy of such an agreement of rights and obligations. Thus, according to F.W. Dillistone,

> the archetypal model in this tradition is simply that of two individuals, each respecting the other's identity yet desiring some closer association with him. The essential pattern of action in such circumstances is that of give and take. Each commits himself to give: each, it follows, expresses his readiness to receive. Each deprives himself of some portion of his own strength or skill or possessions: each receives some valued addition to his own limited resources. While the process of interchange continues all is well. But what happens if one party clings tenaciously to that which he has promised to give? Or snatches more than he is entitled to receive? By such acts he becomes guilty ... That which he has withheld or snatched he must restore in full measure ... Any breaking of covenant obligations must therefore be summarily dealt with according to the uncomplicated law of direct retaliation.[21]

When the divine–human relationship is interpreted in these terms, then God is said to commit himself to providing us with eternal happiness while we in turn commit ourselves to honouring God by living our lives in obedience to his will. However, as

---

[20] John Calvin, *Institutes of the Christian Religion*, II.17.1, trans. Henry Beveridge (London, 1953).

[21] F.W. Dillistone, *The Christian Understanding of Atonement* (London, 1968), 212–13.

sinners we fail to keep our side of the bargain. We do not honour God with our obedience, we transgress the law of God and we live lives that are contrary to his will. In this way we do not give to God what is his right under the covenant agreement, and thereby forfeit our right to eternal happiness. Through our sinful behaviour we become guilty of radically disturbing the balance of rights and obligations between God and ourselves. As I explained in the previous chapter, there are three ways in which this balance can be restored: punishment, satisfaction or condonation. Thus, in the words of H.A. Hodges,

> our relation to God as sinners is this: We must pay a penalty appropriate and adequate to our wrong-doing, we must undergo punishment adequate to our guilt, we must make satisfaction adequate to the affront which we administer to God's honour, and by these means or by direct appeal to his mercy we must propitiate him.[22]

God's justice prevents him from condoning our sins. He cannot take our rebellion lightly as though it does not really seriously damage his rights. Hence an appeal to God's mercy cannot take on the form of a request that he should condone our sins. From his side, God could redress the balance between us by punishment adequate to our guilt. Thus he could withhold from us the eternal happiness to which we would otherwise have been entitled and bestow on us the eternal punishment that we justly deserve. The only way in which we could avoid this fate, would be as yet 'to make satisfaction adequate to the affront which we administer to God's honour'. If this were possible, we could through good works *earn* reinstatement into the covenant agreement that we have broken and again merit the eternal happiness to which we are entitled under the agreement. This would seem to open the way again for a theology of merit in which we can claim the credit for our own salvation rather than saying *Soli Deo Gloria* and giving all the credit to God. As we argued above, the chief advantage of employing a manipulative model is precisely the radical exclusion of this kind of theology.

The way of satisfaction can only allow for a theology of merit on condition that sinners have the *capacity* to make adequate satisfaction. However, since God is infinite, it could be argued that our guilt before him is also infinite. The satisfaction required to restore the balance of rights and duties between God and ourselves, is therefore far beyond our means. Since it is the achievement of Christ that he provided adequate satisfaction in our stead, all the credit for our salvation goes to him and not to us. Salvation still has to be earned, but by Christ rather than by us. *Soli Christo Gloria!* This is the line of argument usually attributed to Anselm, whose theory of atonement is often interpreted as the classical example of a view based on this model. Dillistone summarizes Anselm's position as follows:

> Anselm's diagnosis of the human situation is fundamental to his argument. Man's failure to give due honour to God constitutes a weight, a debt, a doom. If he is to

---

[22] H.A. Hodges, *The Pattern of Atonement* (London, 1955), 45.

be saved from irretrievable disaster he must in some way make satisfaction. Yet it is obvious that this is quite outside his competence. How then can God's original purpose for man be fulfilled? Only if a new man can be found, a man who by perfect obedience can satisfy God's honour himself and by some work of complete supererogation can provide the means of paying the existing debt of his fellows. Such a one was the God-Man. By his unswerving obedience throughout his earthly life he perfectly fulfilled his own obligations as man: by his willing acceptance of death he established such a treasury of merit as would avail to pay the debts of all mankind if they would simply look to him, accept his grace and be saved.[23]

When developed along these lines, this model would seem to provide the basis for a theory of atonement that has all the advantages and none of the disadvantages of the manipulative model of Augustine and Calvin. It avoids a theology of merit without having to turn human beings into objects of divine manipulation. Thereby it can explain how we rather than God are the agents of our own downfall. God can in no way be held responsible for the fact that we have broken our agreements of rights and obligations with him. Finally, this view is able to explain how the work of Christ is essential for restoring the relation between God and ourselves and saving us from eternal punishment: only Christ in his perfect humanity is able to bring about the required satisfaction which is far beyond our means to provide. To him be all thanksgiving and glory! Nevertheless, these advantages are achieved at a price.

First, a theory of penal substitution strikes many of us today as highly immoral since it claims that God punishes the innocent for the transgressions of the guilty.[24] The only way to make some moral sense of this is to interpret it in terms of a feudal concept of honour. God is then viewed as a feudal lord whose honour has been violated by our disobedience. His honour now requires satisfaction, and it does not matter who provides that satisfaction. Thus Christ in his perfect humanity is able to make the adequate satisfaction that is beyond our means to provide. Such feudal honour might have been familiar in the twelfth century, but for most of us today it goes against the grain to look on God as a feudal Lord demanding this kind of honour.

Secondly, one of the reasons why this view of God goes against the grain for us is the following. As I pointed out in previous chapters, people participate in agreements of rights and obligations for the sake of the advantage that each party can gain for him or herself. Under such an agreement I do not value you for who you are but for the services that you are to provide for me, and you too value me merely as a provider of services under the agreement. As such you are not irreplaceable for me, nor am I for you. Anybody else who could provide the same services, would do just as well. If this

---

[23] Dillistone, *The Christian Understanding of Atonement*, 193. For an interpretation of Anselm which brings his view on atonement in many ways more in line with the view that I defend in this and the previous chapter, see David Brown, 'Anselm and atonement', in B. Davies and B. Leftow (eds), *Companion to Anselm* (Cambridge, 2004).

[24] See G.W.H. Lampe, 'The atonement', in A.R. Vidler (ed.), *Soundings. Essays Concerning Christian Understanding* (Cambridge, 1966), 186–7.

is the sort of relationship we have with God, it means that we do not love God for himself alone, but merely as a provider of eternal happiness. To put it crudely: we value heaven more than we value God! On the other hand, God does not love me for myself alone, but merely for the obedience with which I render him honour. To put it crudely: God values my serving his honour more than he values me. For this reason, too, I am replaceable for God by anybody else who is able to satisfy his honour adequately. It does not matter to him whether it is I or Christ in my stead who does so, provided his honour is satisfied. If, as I have argued, the ultimate value of my very existence is bestowed on me by the fact that God loves *me* and not merely my services apart from me, then it is clear that this view entails a concept of God that is radically defective from a religious point of view.

Thirdly, this view on the divine–human relationship cannot account adequately for the nature of divine forgiveness. As I argued in the previous chapter, in an agreement of rights and duties the only alternative for satisfaction or punishment is condonation. In this context, therefore, divine forgiveness can only be viewed as a form of condonation that fails to take sin seriously. In the words of Gustaf Aulén,

> we find in Anselm, as in every form of the Latin theory of Atonement, the alternative stated: *either* a forgiveness of sins by God, which would mean that sin is not treated seriously and so would amount to a toleration of laxity, *or* satisfaction. No other possibility is regarded as conceivable.[25]

In the previous chapter I have explained why such confusion of forgiveness with condonation is mistaken. I will return to this point below.

Fourthly, the account that this theory of atonement provides of the work of Christ can hardly be said to do justice to the unity between the Persons of the Trinity. In this respect it is illuminating to note the way in which St Bernard of Clairvaux distinguishes the *unity* between the Persons of the Trinity from the kind of *union* of love that a believer seeks with God. Unlike the union of love, the unity of the Father and the Son involves an identity of will and essence. This entails that their purpose and attitude toward us should be similarly identical: the purpose and attitude of the Son should be a direct expression of that of the Father. The doctrine of penal substitution presents a very different view of the relationship between the Father and the Son. In the words of David Smith:

> The theory stands in direct and open contradiction to the fundamental article of the Christian faith, that Christ is one with God – one in character and purpose and disposition toward the children of men. It places a gulf between God and Christ, representing God as the stern Judge who insisted on the execution of justice, and Christ as the pitiful Saviour who interposes and satisfies his legal demand and appeases his righteous wrath. They are not one either in their attitudes towards sinners or in the part which they play. God is propitiated, Christ propitiates; God inflicts the punishment, Christ suffers it; God exacts the debt, Christ pays it. This

---

[25] Gustaf Aulén, *Christus Victor* (London, 1953), 105. See also 145–6. 'The Latin theory of atonement' is Aulén's term for all penal substitution theories.

is the fundamental postulate of the theory, God and Christ are not one in character
or purpose or disposition toward sinners.[26]

This does not deny that the Father *agrees* with the Son adopting the 'character or
purpose or disposition toward sinners' that he does. However, 'agreeing' does not
amount to 'sharing'. In terms of Bernard's distinction, 'there must be at least two
wills for there to be agreement'. Agreement between the Father and the Son would
account for no more that a 'union of wills' and not for the 'unity of will' which
constitutes the unity between the Father and the Son.[27]

Fifthly, this view contradicts the patristic intuition that atonement is something
done *by* God and not *to* God. Thus Aulén argues that on this view God is no longer the
direct agent of atonement. It is Christ in his humanity who makes satisfaction to God.
'The satisfaction must be made by man; and this is precisely what is done in Christ's
atoning work … For Anselm the central problem is: 'Where can a man be found, free
from sin and guilt, and able to offer himself as an acceptable sacrifice to God?'[28] It is
on this point that Aulén rejects Anselm's 'Latin theory' of atonement in favour of
what he calls the 'Classical theory' of Irenaeus who 'does not think of the atonement
as an offering made to God by Christ from man's side, or as it were from below; for
God remains throughout the effective agent in the work of redemption'.[29] It is true
that Anselm and his followers claimed that God 'gives' or 'sends' Christ to act as
Mediator. In this sense God is the initiator or author of the Atonement but he is not the
agent who carries it out. The agent of the Atonement is Christ in his humanity.

Finally, penal substitution satisfies the demands of retributive justice. As I pointed
out in the previous chapter, retributive justice merely removes guilt but it does not
restore fellowship. Sin is seen here as guilt rather than as estrangement. Salvation
through penal substitution is therefore the removal of guilt rather than reconciliation
with God that overcomes estrangement. In this sense the theory of penal substitution
is not a theory of atonement (in the sense of 'at-one-ment') at all. If we look on sin as
estrangement from God, we will need a theory of atonement that explains how we can
be reconciled with the God from whom we have become estranged. My suggestion is
that such a theory should be developed along the lines suggested in the previous
chapter.

Atonement as Reconciliation

A doctrine of atonement explaining how we can be reconciled with God must assume
that God is a God of love who seeks restorative rather than retributive justice in his

---

[26] David Smith, *The Atonement in the Light of History and the Modern Spirit* (London, 1918), 106.

[27] On St Bernard's distinction see his *Serious Song of Songs*, 4 vols (Kalamazoo, MI, 1971–80), sermon
71. I return to this point in more detail in Chapter 6.

[28] Aulén, *Christus Victor*, 103.

[29] Aulén, *Christus Victor*, 50.

relation to us. God always remains willing to forgive and to pay the price of forgiveness. The sacrifice required for reconciliation is the sacrifice made by God. Thus D.M. Baillie points out that in the New Testament the sacrificial system of ancient Israel 'is completely transformed into the idea of an atonement in which *God alone bears the cost*'.[30] He would rather suffer at our hands than to turn his back on us.

This view on atonement runs contrary to the ancient doctrine of divine impassibility according to which divine perfection entails that God lacks nothing and therefore can have no desires that could be thwarted, causing him to suffer. This view of divine perfection is part of the inheritance of Platonism and was self-evident for the Fathers and for a vast number of theologians in the Christian tradition.[31] It would seem that the doctrine of penal substitution is more compatible with this traditional doctrine since it does not attribute the suffering required for our salvation to God but to Christ in his human nature. However this would turn God into a quietist who avoids vulnerability and suffering by renouncing all desires. This would not be the God of love who forgives us our trespasses and *desires* that we attain ultimate happiness by being reconciled with him.[32] It is understandable that in contemporary theology most theologians seem to have very little difficulty in rejecting the doctrine of divine impassibility. As Ronald Goetz points out, 'the rejection of the ancient doctrine of divine impassibility has become a theological commonplace'.[33]

As I explained in the previous chapter, divine forgiveness is a necessary but not a sufficient condition for our reconciliation with God. Such reconciliation also requires penitence and a change of heart on our part. In order to be reconciled with God we need to change from rebels against God who seek ultimate happiness in finite goods, to children of God who seek our ultimate happiness in the kind of fellowship in which we identify with God by seeking his will as our own. To be reconciled with God I need to abandon the 'I' that turns his back on God and become the 'I' that desires to live in loving fellowship with God.

Since loving fellowship is a personal relation between free agents who freely initiate their own actions, we can only achieve such fellowship with God through our own free choice. God cannot bring about this change in us in a manipulative way that excludes our own responsible agency. God can enable us to turn to him by removing the many obstacles that prevent us from doing so, but he cannot cause our response to his love. Are Augustine and Calvin not right in their fears that this view entails a theology of merit in which we can claim some of the credit for our own salvation? I

---

[30] Baillie, *God was in Christ* (London, 1961), 175.

[31] Marcel Sarot has pointed out that among the Fathers even the defenders of patripassionism and theopaschitism in fact paid respect to this doctrine. See Marcel Sarot, 'Patripassionism, theopaschitism and the suffering of God: some historical and terminological considerations', *Religious Studies*, 26 (1990), 363–75. For an exhaustive discussion and detailed assessment of the conceptual price of either accepting or rejecting this traditional doctrine, see Marcel Sarot, *God, Passibility and Corporeality* (Kampen, 1992).

[32] On this see my *The Model of Love* (Cambridge, 1993), sections 9.3 and 9.4.

[33] Ronald Goetz, 'The suffering of God', *The Christian Century*, 103 (1986), 385.

have tried to show that this will only be the case if we were to interpret our relationship with God as an agreement of rights and obligations in which we earn our right to divine salvation by fulfilling our covenant obligations to God. In a relationship of loving fellowship this is excluded because love and forgiveness can never be earned or merited, but by definition remains a free gift of grace.

In the previous chapter I have discussed the many obstacles that prevent us from freely turning to God. In order to attain loving fellowship with God we will have to depend on the grace of God to remove these obstacles and thus to enable us freely to respond to his love. Let me conclude this chapter by briefly summarizing the obstacles that God in his grace will have to remove in order for us to be reconciled with him.

1   Our estrangement from God has made us ignorant of the very fact that we have become estranged. We have lost our Socratic self-knowledge and are fundamentally mistaken about the true nature of our daimon. Like the prodigal son in the far country we are in fact for the moment quite satisfied with our state of estrangement and see no reason for abandoning it. We can therefore only repent and change our ways if God would make us aware of our estrangement and like the prodigal son face up to the fact that our search for ultimate happiness by craving finite riches and fame rather than by doing the will of our Father is bound to fail and has to be abandoned.

2   Estrangement from God has not only made us ignorant about ourselves, but also ignorant about God. We cannot repent because we do not know whom we have offended. Therefore, God will have to make himself known to us as the God of love who desires us to be reconciled with him and has paid the price of forgiveness in order to enable us to be reconciled if only we would respond to his love by repentance and a change of heart. This is the Good News of the love of God that constrains us to respond to it in our lives (2 Corinthians 5:14).

3   If we are to attain ultimate happiness through loving identification with the will of God, he should make his will known to us. We must receive the gift of enlightenment in order to know his will before we can lead our lives accordingly.

4   But enlightenment is not enough. Knowing the will of God does not entail our having the power or the ability to live according to it. Hence God should also grant us the gift of empowerment that will enable us to live our lives consistently in accordance with his will.

5   Doing the will of God will as such does not make us ultimately happy. We can only be happy if we do so joyfully out of love and not merely out of duty because we have to. For this we need what St. Bernard calls the gift of 'wisdom' or 'taste'. We need to be inspired with a taste for the good in order to find happiness in doing so.

Bestowing these five gifts on us constitutes the fundamental saving acts by which God opens the way for us to repent and be reconciled with him. It is in these saving acts that God makes himself known to us. It is only in his acts in relation to us that we come to know who he is. It is now clear that, if the doctrine of atonement is to be understood as an explanation of God's acts of salvation, then it is the essential point of departure for understanding the doctrines of Christology and the Trinity that aim at explaining who God is. In this light we can now turn to an examination of these doctrines.

CHAPTER 5

The Doctrine of Christology

Atonement and Christology

For the Fathers it was their views on salvation that provided the grounds for their claim that Christ was both divine and human. Thus the divinity of Christ follows from the claim that only God can save: 'The underlying conviction of the genuinely religious man about salvation is that its source can only be God himself. This fundamental axiom was a basic criterion of orthodox thought in all the great fourth- and fifth-century controversies.'[1] This axiom was entailed by their views on salvation. Thus according to the recapitulation theory only a truly divine saviour could save: 'Only one who was divine in his own right could impart to man a share in his own divine nature, make them "partakers of the divine nature" (2 Peter 1:4).'[2] Similarly the ransom theory entailed that Christ should be fully divine. If he were merely human he could not have been victorious over the devil. The devil is able to hold a mere human in captivity but he cannot prevail over one who is divine. This also applied to all sacrificial views on atonement (including the later theory of penal substitution). Only a divine sacrifice could provide adequate satisfaction to the infinite honour and justice of God. From this it is clear why the Fathers could appeal to their views on salvation to reject all attempts to deny or to limit the divinity of Christ. This provided Athanasius with a knock-down argument against the view of Arius that Christ is a created being: created beings cannot be saved by one who is himself merely a created being.

Thus the patristic ideas on salvation entailed the divinity of Christ. But divinity is not enough. Their ideas on salvation also required them to claim the full humanity of Christ. Apart from the axiom that 'only God can save', their ideas on salvation entailed a second axiom that Gregory of Nazianzus formulated as follows: 'What Christ has not assumed he has not healed.' Thus the recapitulation theory entailed that if Christ did not assume our full human nature he could not make us fully divine by making us partake fully in his divine nature. Similarly, the ransom and sacrificial theories entailed the full humanity of Christ since only a fully human Christ could provide a ransom or a sacrifice in our stead. The claim that Christ was fully human follows not only from the very human picture of Jesus presented in the New Testament, but also from the views on salvation held by the Fathers. This provided them with a knock-down argument against all attempts to deny or to limit the full humanity of Christ. Thus Irenaeus and Tertullian could counter the Gnostic view that Christ's human existence was mere appearance rather than reality by arguing that in

---

[1] Maurice Wiles, *The Making of Christian Doctrine* (Cambridge, 1967), 95.
[2] Maurice Wiles, *The Christian Fathers* (London, 1977), 41.

order to save us Christ had to really become what we are, giving his body for our body and his soul for our soul, and Origen could argue that 'the whole man would not have been saved unless Christ had not taken upon himself the whole man'. Later this same argument was also the basis for the Antiochene rejection of the claim by Apollinarius that Christ did not have a human soul. Without assuming a human soul Christ could only save our bodies but not our souls. He gave his body for our bodies and his soul for our souls.

The Fathers' views on salvation thus required them to confess both the complete divinity and the complete humanity of Christ. It is obvious that this confession raised serious conceptual difficulties for the Fathers. If Christ is to be truly divine, then he must have had all the necessary characteristics of divinity. He must then have been omniscient, omnipotent, omnipresent and impassible. However, this makes it very difficult to uphold his true humanity since that would entail all the limitations inherent in human existence. If he were truly human, he must really have been subject to hunger, thirst, weariness, ignorance, temptation and suffering as, in fact, the New Testament describes him to be. How, then, can we conceive of such mutually exclusive natures as humanity and divinity being ascribed to one and the same being? The Fathers agreed that it would be heretical to remove this incoherence by denying or limiting either the divinity or the humanity of Christ. To some it seemed that the only alternative was somehow to ascribe the divinity and the humanity to two distinct 'subjects' in Christ. Thus for example Diodore of Tarsus in the fourth century was led to distinguish between Jesus as the Son of God and as the Son of David, and to ascribe divinity to the one and humanity to the other. A solution along these lines, which generally found favour with theologians of the Antiochene school, seemed to do inadequate justice to the unity of Christ and was therefore firmly rejected by the school of Alexandria. This difference came to a head in the fifth century with the controversy between Nestorius of Constantinople who defended the Antiochene line, and Cyril of Alexandria who upheld the Alexandrian objections. This controversy was very confusing to say the least. J.N.D. Kelly warns us 'that at no phase in the evolution of the Church's theology have the fundamental issues been so mixed up with the clash of politics and personalities'.[3] In the end Nestorianism was declared a heresy, even though, as Kelly points out, 'when we try to assess the character of Nestorius's teaching, one thing which is absolutely clear is that he was not a Nestorian in the classic sense of the word'.[4] This bitter controversy presented a serious threat to the unity of the Church. In an attempt to reconcile the feuding parties and restore unity, the emperor Marcian convened an ecumenical synod at Chalcedon in 451 in order to produce a compromise. This resulted in the Christological settlement laid down in the Chalcedonian Definition.

The central question was how 'one and the same' Christ (a phrase repeated five times in the definition) could simultaneously be both divine and human.

---

[3] J.N.D. Kelly, *Early Christian Doctrine* (London, 1977), 310.
[4] Kelly, *Early Christian Doctrine*, 316.

The Chalcedonian response was to distinguish between the two 'natures' (*physeis*) which concur 'without confusion, without change, without division, without separation' in one 'Person' (*hypostasis* or *prosopon*). However, this seems to be merely a verbal rather than a substantive solution since the Chalcedonian definition fails to provide a precise definition of these terms. Thus Sarah Coakley points out that

> the relatively *undefined* character of the key terms 'nature' (*physis*) and 'person' (*hypostasis*) in the so-called Definition ... draws attention to the open-endedness of the document, its unclarity about the precise meaning of key terms. If anything is 'defined' in the 'Definition' it is not these crucial concepts. To be sure, these terms had a pre-history, but it was an ambiguous one and the 'Definition' does not clear up the ambiguity.[5]

Nevertheless, the Chalcedonian Definition did provide a normative guideline for the Church in all its subsequent attempts to understand the Christological issues. Although it did not itself provide such an understanding, it laid down the limits within which such an understanding should be sought. It did this by (1) reaffirming in its preamble the acts of salvation detailed at Nicaea and Constantinople; (2) laying down the limits which should not be transgressed if these acts of salvation are to be affirmed; (3) rejecting all those views put forward in the preceding controversies that transgressed these limits, and (4) remaining open-ended enough to allow for any understanding that could be developed within these limits.

The significance of the Chalcedonian Definition was therefore regulative rather than substantive. It regulated Christological thinking by defining its limits. Since the terms in which it did so were left relatively undefined, the limits it set remained open-ended and left room for a large variety of views. This was a good thing because it remains doubtful whether the terms used by Chalcedon were themselves suitable for producing a substantive and coherent solution for the Christological issues.

Natures or Functions?

At the time, the Chalcedonian Definition was the best resolution of the Christological issues that the Fathers could produce, given the limitations of the conceptual apparatus of Platonism that, as we have seen, determined their way of thinking. This way of thinking was based on the distinction between the phenomena of our experience and the eternal essences or natures that lay behind them. It was to these essences or natures, approached not by experience but by a process of speculative reasoning, that the highest reality and the highest value were ascribed: 'The fact that patristic theology grew up against such a background gave to it an ontological urge and an ontological confidence which are both its glory and its

---

[5] Sarah Coakley, 'What does Chalcedon solve and what does it not? Some reflections on the status and meaning of the Chalcedonian "Definition"', in Stephen T. Davis, Daniel Kendall and Gerald O'Collins (eds), *The Incarnation* (Oxford, 2002), 148.

weakness.'[6] In the previous chapter we saw how the Platonic conceptual apparatus determined the patristic understanding of salvation. This way of thinking also led the Fathers to understand the incarnation in terms of the relation between the eternal human and divine natures of Christ. Since the way in which the Fathers tended to define these eternal natures made them logically incompatible, understanding the incarnation turned into an insoluble logical puzzle. How could one and the same being participate in two such incompatible natures? Their attempts to solve this puzzle led to a variety of clumsy and convoluted speculative hypotheses. Did Christ have only one will and/or one mind? Or did he have both a divine and a human mind and/or will?[7] And how were these two minds and/or wills related? Was Christ's divine nature eliminated or somehow suppressed while he was incarnate? Or did his divine nature override his human nature at the time? If Christ had both a human body and a human soul, how was the human soul related to the Divine Word that was incarnate in him? Such speculative hypotheses either subject the divine nature of Christ to his human nature or his human to his divine nature. Or else they try to maintain both at the same time by turning Christ into a kind of divine–human schizophrenic. The Chalcedonian Definition set the limits within which these questions were asked but it failed to answer any of them. Thus William Temple concluded that 'the Definition represents the bankruptcy of Greek patristic thought; it marks the definite failure of all attempts to explain the Incarnation in terms of Essence, Substance, Nature and the like'.[8]

Such ontological speculations, as well as the Platonic frame of thought that gave rise to them, must sound very strange to ordinary believers today. They may still be of interest to logically minded philosophers who revel in logical puzzles, but the average believer in the pew today is 'empirically' minded and therefore more interested in the phenomena of experience than in ontological speculations about eternal essences. Believers are interested in the ways in which Christ relates to them personally and the role he plays in reconciling them to God rather than in ontological speculations about the inner workings of his eternal nature or his psychological make-up: 'To speak of God in himself, abstracted from our apprehension of him in a relationship of faith and adoration, suggests a detached, spectator attitude, a knowledge of the head rather than of the heart.'[9]

A relational approach 'of the heart' is also closer to the way the Bible talks about Christ. The New Testament tells us about what Christ did and what difference that makes to our relations to God and to one another. It does not provide us with speculative theories about his inner nature. Thus Oscar Cullmann argues that

> when it is asked in the New Testament 'who is Christ?', the question never means exclusively, or even primarily, 'What is his nature?' but first of all, 'What is his

---

[6] Wiles, *The Making of Christian Doctrine*, 117–18.

[7] For a contemporary resuscitation of the two minds hypothesis, see Thomas V. Morris, *The Logic of God Incarnate* (Ithaca, NY, 1986).

[8] William Temple, *Christus Veritas* (London, 1924), 134.

[9] Maurice Wiles, *The Remaking of Christian Doctrine* (London, 1974), 26.

function?' ... As a result of the necessity of combating the heretics, the Church fathers subordinated the interpretation of the person and the work of Christ to the question of the 'natures'. In any case their emphases, compared to those of the New Testament, were misplaced. Even when they did speak of the work of Christ, they did so only in connection with discussion about his nature. Even if this shifting of emphasis was necessary against certain heretical views, the discussion of 'natures' is nonetheless ultimately a Greek, not a Jewish or Biblical problem.[10]

It is clear that the Platonic tools used by the Fathers are woefully inadequate for the task at hand. Not only did they create problems that could not be solved without resorting to convoluted and clumsy speculative constructions, but they were also very far removed from both our contemporary forms of thought and from the way in which the Bible talks about Christ. But then, as Montefiore points out, 'there is nothing sacrosanct about the philosophical categories of the patristic period. God did not reveal to us a particular philosophy: he revealed himself to us in Jesus Christ.'[11] Maybe we should take leave of the Platonic ontology and, rather, follow up Cullmann's suggestion that we develop a more 'functional' Christology. Instead of producing speculative theories about Christ's inner nature, we should rest content with talk about what we receive through him. We then have to ask what role Christ plays in reconciling us with God and in what sense this role entails both his divinity and his humanity. In answering these questions we can come to understand the meaning of St Paul's claim that 'God was in Christ reconciling the world to himself' (2 Corinthians 5:19).

Reconciliation and the Divinity of Christ

In previous chapters I have argued that our estrangement from God has made us ignorant both of God and of ourselves. We have lost our Socratic self-knowledge. We no longer know our true daimon. Like the prodigal son, we live in the illusion that we can find ultimate happiness in striving after finite goods rather than in enjoying the loving fellowship of God. But even if we were to seek this fellowship by making God's will for us our own, we are unable to do so because we do not know what his will for us is. This is the first obstacle that prevents us from seeking repentance and a change of heart. However, we have not only become ignorant about ourselves, but also about God. We no longer know him as the loving Father who desires that we return his love and find our ultimate happiness in his fellowship. We no longer know that for the sake

---

[10] Oscar Cullmann, *The Christology of the New Testament* (London, 1959), 3f. 'It was often the heretic who determined the general lines along which doctrine should develop; it was he who chose the ground on which the doctrinal battles were to be fought. Frequently indeed he chose not only the ground for the battle but also the weapons to be used in it' (Wiles, *The Making of Christian Doctrine*, 33). See pages 28–36 for Wiles's illustrations of this point.

[11] H.W. Montefiore, 'Towards a Christology for today', in A.R. Vidler (ed.), *Soundings. Essays Concerning Christian Understanding* (Cambridge, 1966), 157.

of reconciling us with him, he is willing to forgive us and to pay the price of forgiveness. This is the second reason why we are unable to repent and turn to God:

> The tragedy of the human situation lies in the fact that sinful man has lost the knowledge of the God against whom he has sinned and that *this is the punishment* which sin can never escape … The sins of men have built their own prison … They *cannot* repent, because they do not know whom they have offended.[12]

It is clearly a necessary condition for our reconciliation with God that he should free us from our ignorance and reveal to us both who we are and who he is. It is this that God has done in Christ: 'The character, acts and teaching of Jesus, are seen as God's own revelatory and loving acts for our salvation.'[13] In Jesus God makes himself known to us as a loving God who desires our fellowship and is willing to pay the price of forgiveness in order to win it. Anyone who has seen Jesus has seen the Father (John 14:9). In this respect Jesus is 'very God'. In Jesus God also reveals his will to us in order that we may be enabled to identify with him in fellowship by making his will our own and living our lives accordingly. Thus 'Christology is not only concerned with Christ as the human face of God, but also with Christ as the pattern of what man was meant to be. The will of God for the world and for man comes to expression in the incarnate one.'[14] In this respect Jesus is also 'very man'.

Which aspects of 'the character, acts and teaching of Jesus' are manifestations of his divinity and which express his humanity? In the history of theology this question has not always been answered in the same way. Thus for Tertullian 'the divine nature is reflected in the miracles, the human nature in the sufferings'.[15] This view was generally shared by the Fathers and is entailed by their Platonic view of God as an omnipotent, omniscient, immutable, self-sufficient and impassible transcendent being. Accordingly, the suffering of Jesus cannot be a manifestation of his divinity but typically expresses his humanity. However, as I argued in Chapter 3, reconciliation with God assumes God to be a loving God who desires our reconciliation and is willing to pay the price of forgiveness. But then it is especially the suffering of Jesus that expresses the divine nature. As D.M. Baillie points out, 'it is the love of God himself that is seen in the suffering of Christ. In the New Testament the love of Christ and the love of God are the same thing: the two phrases are interchangeable (see Romans 8:35, 38f).'[16] It is at this point above all that the doctrine of 'homo-ousios' makes sense: 'to acknowledge with the Creed that our Lord is of one substance with the Father, is to acknowledge that what God gave in the giving of his Son was *himself*'.[17]

---

[12] John Burnaby, *Christian Words and Christian Meanings* (London, 1955), 94–5.

[13] Brian Hebblethwaite, *The Incarnation. Collected Essays in Christology* (Cambridge, 1987), 63.

[14] Hebblethwaite, *The Incarnation*, 151.

[15] Wiles, *The Christian Fathers*, 59.

[16] D.M. Baillie, *God Was in Christ* (London, 1961), 68.

[17] John Burnaby, *The Belief of Christendom*, 76. Compare Baillie's statement that 'the love of Jesus is the love of God in a sense which makes nonsense of Arianism' (*God was in Christ*, 69).

Here Brian Hebblethwaite makes a useful distinction between 'liberal and orthodox Christianity':

> it is the difference between the view that God 'acted' supremely through the man Jesus and the view that the human life and death of Jesus were supremely God's own 'acts' for our salvation ... To say that the acts of Jesus *were* the acts of God incarnate is to assert the 'homo-ousion'.[18]

But then Jesus is 'of one substance' (homo-ousios) with the Father in a functional rather than in the ontological sense assumed by the Fathers. His unity with the Father is a unity of agency rather than a unity of Platonic 'nature'. On the 'liberal' view, however, there is no such unity of agency since Jesus becomes merely a human intermediary or representative through whom God acts. On the view of atonement I have defended above, the person who forgives is the person who has to pay the price for reconciliation. This cannot be done by someone else as a representative acting on behalf of the person who forgives. Since in restoring our fellowship with God, it is God who forgives, it is also God himself who has to pay the price and has to absorb into his own suffering the consequences of the wrong that we have done to him. On Calvary God reveals to us the cost of his forgiveness. Furthermore, since forgiveness is by definition unconditional, the suffering of Jesus cannot be seen as merely the condition for God's forgiveness. It is, rather, the direct expression of this forgiveness and the price God has to pay for it. In this way I can understand Hebblethwaite's categorical statement 'that God's forgiving love does not depend on the death of Christ, but rather is manifested and enacted in it'.[19] But then Jesus cannot be a human representative whose suffering fulfils on our behalf the conditions necessary for God to forgive (as is implied by substitutionary theories of atonement), nor can he be a representative who pays the price for divine forgiveness on God's behalf. On the contrary, as Hebblethwaite correctly point out, 'the suffering and Cross of Jesus can be seen as God's own suffering and Cross in the world'.[20] For these reasons we cannot claim that the cross of Jesus is the manifestation and enactment of divine forgiveness without at the same time affirming the divinity of Jesus.

But this is not all. Christ's suffering is not merely the *revelation* of the price for forgiveness that God has to pay. I have argued that such a revelation is also a *necessary condition* for this forgiveness to achieve reconciliation. On this view Wiles[21] is correct that the passion is not merely 'exhibitive' but also 'performative'. The 'exhibition' is itself a 'performance' effecting a necessary condition for reconciliation: 'The saving action of incarnation – to the point of crucifixion – has revealed that previously unknown love, and the effect of this revelation is to be the

---

[18] Hebblethwaite, *The Incarnation*, 69.

[19] Hebblethwaite, *The Incarnation*, 37.

[20] Hebblethwaite, *The Incarnation*, 64.

[21] Wiles, *Remaking of Christian Doctrine*, 80. In this way the view I am defending does not fall prey to the weaknesses of so-called 'subjective' views of the atonement. On this point see also A.G. McGrath, 'Soteriology', in *The Blackwell Encyclopedia of Modern Christian Thought* (Oxford, 1993), 623–4.

transformation of the loveless into the lovely.'[22] In this respect Christ's suffering on Calvary is a necessary condition for our salvation. By revealing his love for us here, we come to know God and the way is opened for us to enjoy his loving fellowship. Fellowship requires that we know each other as persons in the sense that we adopt an attitude of mutual trust and open candour in relation to each other.[23] If ultimate happiness consists of being in the love of God, it follows that we can only be ultimately happy to the extent that we know God in this way: 'This is eternal life: to know you the only true God, and Jesus Christ whom you have sent' (John 17:3).

The divinity of Jesus, then, is manifested in his suffering and his cross. For the Fathers, however, the divinity of Jesus was usually connected with his miracles and especially with the resurrection. These were taken as signs of the divine omnipotence and omniscience in which he transcended the limitations of human existence. The trouble with this view is that it tends to suggest a docetism in which the divinity of Jesus is conceived of in a way that excludes his true humanity. The problem for the Fathers was therefore to avoid this docetism by reconciling their conception of divinity with the humanity of Jesus. In order to be truly human, Jesus must have been subject to the limitations of human existence. It is therefore incoherent to claim that he is truly human and then to interpret his divinity in ways that contradict this claim. Hebblethwaite is right in affirming that

> in no way do we follow the 'docetic' tendencies of early Christianity, which found it hard to believe, for example, that Jesus shared the limitations of human psychology and cognition. This is to say that for Christian belief the Incarnation involved God's subjecting himself to the limitations of real humanity in order to achieve his purposes of revelation and reconciliation.[24]

The divinity of Jesus should therefore be understood in ways that are manifested *within* the limits of his true humanity and are not contrary to it. The abilities and the knowledge of Jesus were divine in the sense that he made a divine use of them within the limits of his humanity and not in the sense that they were not subjected to these limits: 'What did Jesus know? He knew, initially, what a village boy learned, who listened to the Rabbis, and made the best use of his opportunities. But of this knowledge, scanty as we should think it, he made a divinely perfect use.'[25] Elsewhere Farrer argues that the supposition that the power and knowledge of Jesus were divine in a sense that transcended the limits of human existence

> not only conflicts with the evidence in the Gospels, it conflicts no less with the very possibility of genuine incarnation. Christ is very God, indeed, but also very man; and an omniscient being who knows all the answers before he thinks and all the futures before he acts is not a man at all, he has escaped the human

[22] Hebblethwaite, *The Incarnation*, 1.
[23] See my *The Model of Love* (Cambridge, 1993), 179–81.
[24] Hebblethwaite, *The Incarnation*, 22. See also 164.
[25] Austin Farrer, *The Brink of Mystery* (London, 1976), 20.

predicament … On the other hand, he *knows how* to be the Son of God in the several situations of his gradually unfolding destiny, and in the way appropriate to each. He is tempted to depart from that knowledge, but he resists the temptation. And that suffices for the incarnation to be real. For 'being the Son of God' is the exercise of a sort of life; and in order to exercise it he must know how to exercise that life: it is a question of practical knowledge.[26]

Thus, Jesus was divine in the sense that his life (and his death) revealed to us the love of God, and his knowledge and power were such that he *knew how* to live this life and had the ability to do so within the limits of human existence.

The limits of humanity to which Jesus was subjected, were twofold. First, there were the limits inherent to finite human existence: limits to what humans can do and to what they can know and the limits to life that go with mortality. If Jesus was truly human he must have been subject to these limits. He could not have been omnipotent and omniscient in the sense he was taken to be so in patristic theology. Secondly, there were the limits given by the specific historical circumstances of a human life. Thus, Jesus was not a human-being-in-general (the universal human 'nature' of Platonism) but a specific human person living at a specific time and place. In the words of Austin Farrer:

this was how God's love was shown to be utterly divine – in accepting every circumstance of our manhood. He spared himself nothing. He was not a copybook man-in-general, he was a Galilean carpenter, a free-lance rabbi; and he wove up his life, as each of us must, out of the materials that were to hand.[27]

The divinity of Jesus did not override the limits of his humanity, but manifested itself *within* these limits.

In brief then, Jesus was a *real* human being subject to all the limitations of human existence. Within these limits, however, he was 'very God' in the sense that the forgiving love of God was revealed to us in his life and especially in his death on the cross. Through this revelation we come to know God and can be reconciled with him.

Reconciliation and the Humanity of Christ

Jesus was

a 'weak' human being like ourselves, who had to eat and drink, who got tired, so also he was a man who had to submit to the will of God, who had to struggle, who was 'in all points tempted like as we are,' a man who we see asking God, listening to God, praying to God, thanking God, one who was neither omniscient nor omnipotent. His soul could be 'sorrowful unto death'; he could tremble and faint, and plead with God to remove from him the bitter cup of suffering. He was a man

---

[26] Austin Farrer, *Interpretation and Belief* (London, 1976), 135.

[27] Austin Farrer, *A Celebration of Faith* (London, 1970), 89.

who lived as a Jew in the late period of the ancient world; who shared the views of his time, and expressed himself in the language of his people; in brief, in the full sense of the word, he was an historical personality.[28]

In this sense Jesus was *really* human.

He was, however, more than really human. He was also *perfectly* human. He was the paradigm of human perfection. For this reason God does not in the incarnation merely reveal to us who he is, but also who we are. By revealing to us in Jesus what it means to live in his fellowship, it becomes clear to us how far we have strayed from this ideal and have failed to realize our daimon in life. As I have argued above, this revelation is the second necessary condition for our reconciliation with God. We cannot identify in love with God by making his will our own if we do not know what his will for us is. For this reason Jesus was not only 'very God' but also 'very man'. We might say that he was not only an 'icon' of God but also an 'icon' of true humanity.

Icons are holy images that play an important role in Orthodox liturgy and spirituality. As such they are very different from mere pretty pictures. They are literally 'representations' in the sense that for the believer they 're-present' or make present anew some saint or archangel or the Virgin Mary with the child Jesus. It is something like the large photograph of my long dead grandmother that used to hang in my mother's bedroom. It was not merely a pretty picture but a representation that made one think of granny and thus experience her presence even though she was long departed. So, too, it is with icons. In the presence of the icon, believers experience the presence of the saint. Icons are images with a double significance.

Icon is the Greek word for an image and as such it also occurs in the Bible. Thus already on the first page of Genesis we read in the Greek translation: 'Then God said, "Let us make human beings in our image, as our *icon*, to have dominion over the fish of the sea, the birds of the air, the cattle, all wild animals on the land, and everything that creeps on the earth"' (Genesis 1:26). We are created as *icons* of God in the sense that God's dominion is re-presented in our dominion over the earth and especially over the powers of evil that tend to estrange us from God. God rules creation in what we as his *icons* are called upon to do in our lives.

Our lives can only be *icons* of God's dominion if we live in loving fellowship with God and make his will our own. In our state of estrangement, however, we rule, but not as *icons* of God's rule. In the things we do, God's Kingdom is not realized. We tend rather to replace the *icon* of God's dominion with that of ourselves. All too often the words of Romans 1:22–3 apply to us: 'They boast of their wisdom, but they have made fools of themselves, exchanging the glory of the immortal God for an *icon* shaped like a mortal man, even for *icons* like birds, beasts and reptiles.' It is significant that the birds, beasts and creepy-crawlies of Genesis 1 return here – but then as those who have dominion and not those who are subjected to the dominion of

---

[28] Emil Brunner, *The Mediator* (London, 1934), 363–4.

God! Our dominion is foolish because it is not an *icon* of God's dominion. For this reason God has again revealed his dominion to us in Jesus as 'the *icon* of the invisible God, the first-born of all creation' (Colossians 1:15). In him we see again what it means to live in fellowship with God. He is the first-born in whose likeness the whole of Creation is to be reborn. The community of believers is therefore 'predestined to be conformed to the *icon* of his Son, in order that he might be the first-born among many brethern' (Romans 8:29). In this way the life and death of Jesus is for us the *icon* of true humanity in the fellowship of God. It is him who we are to emulate if we are to find our ultimate happiness in the love of God.

The aim of Christian ethics is the realization of God's purposes for us by making these purposes our own. In this connection the significance of the incarnation is that God's purposes for us are not revealed merely in a set of commandments but in the person of Jesus whose paradigmatic example we are to follow if we are to attain ultimate happiness in the fellowship of God.[29] The Christian life is one in which we are to become Christ-like through the *imitatio Christi*. The primary focus of this *imitatio* is that we should relate to God in the way that Jesus did. Thus the Christian life is one of obedience to God in the way Jesus was obedient (Philippians 2:8, 12). This was the obedience of love and not merely the obedience of duty. Jesus did the will of God because through love he had made God's will his own and not merely because he subjected himself dutifully to the divine law. This obedience through love is expressed especially in the prayers of Jesus in which his love of God brings him to say 'Father, if it be your will, take this cup from me. Yet not my will but yours be done.' (Luke 22:42). The prayers of Jesus manifest the way in which he relates to God and therefore express his perfect humanity. His life and death manifest the effects of this way of relating to God and therefore the effects of the perfect humanity that we are to emulate in the *imitatio Christi*.

In this way we can understand his miracles as the effects of his perfect human fellowship with God and hence as the manifestation of his perfect humanity rather than as proof of his divinity, as maintained by the Fathers. According to D.M. Baillie:

> the problem of the 'mighty works' can be disposed of neither by denying them out of hand as unhistorical, nor by accepting them as sheerly supernatural portents because a divine Christ can do anything, but is to be met only by regarding them as works of faith, wrought by the power of God in response to human faith for which all things are possible.[30]

Baillie rejects the traditional tendency to interpret the 'signs and wonders' of Jesus as proofs of his divinity since this interpretation is

> quite at variance with the mind of our Lord himself. He condemned the desire to have 'signs and wonders' as a basis for faith, and he plainly thought of his works

---

[29] For an interesting discussion of this point see Linda Zagzebski, 'The incarnation and virtue ethics', in Stephen T. Davis, Daniel Kendall and Gerald O'Collins (eds), *The Incarnation* (Oxford, 2002), 313–31.

[30] D.M. Baillie, *God was in Christ*, 13.

> as manifestations of God's love and power which are at the disposal of all men if they will believe. They are works of God's power but they are also works of human faith ... Thus the miracles of our Lord are regarded as 'signs' of the Kingdom because they were works of human faith in God, through which 'the powers of the world to come' are brought right into the conditions of human life on earth.[31]

This applies especially to the resurrection of Christ in which above all he, as the new Adam, is the 'first-born' of all humanity (Colossians 1:15, 18). The widely spread Adam Christology of first-generation Christianity 'presented the risen Christ as the prototype of a new mankind, eldest brother of the eschatological family of God'.[32] The resurrection of Christ is therefore the supreme manifestation of the renewal of life in the loving fellowship of God. We may share in this life if we follow him and become renewed in his image.

In Jesus, this perfect humanity in the fellowship of God is manifested within the limits of human finitude and historical situatedness. This determines what it means for us to be followers of Jesus. We are not called upon to emulate him by living the life of a first-century Galilean carpenter and freelance rabbi. *Imitatio Christi* should not be understood as an attempt to imitate the historical details of Jesus' life and actions.[33] On the contrary, we are called upon to identify in love with the will of God in the way he did and thus to emulate his moral and spiritual perfection within the limits *of our own* finitude and historical situation. In this sense the character, acts and teaching of Jesus manifest the true and ideal humanity which God wills that each of us should emulate in his or her own situation. In revealing this to us through the perfect humanity of Jesus, God enables us to identify with him in loving fellowship and thus to become reconciled with him.

In this chapter I have argued, on the one hand, that for the Christian believer Jesus is 'very God' in the sense that he is the paradigmatic revelation of God's love for us and of God's willingness to pay the price for reconciliation with us. On the other hand, Jesus is also 'very man' for the believer, in the sense that he is the paradigmatic revelation of human perfection in the fellowship of God that believers are called upon to emulate in order to attain ultimate happiness. By this dual revelation Jesus opens the way for us to be reconciled with God.

But this is not the whole story. God's action in reconciling the world to himself involves all three persons of the Trinity and not only the incarnate Son. In what sense, then, does the view on divine reconciliation defended above entail a Trinitarian theology?

---

[31] Baillie, *God was in Christ*, 13–14.

[32] James D.G. Dunn, *Christology in the Making* (London, 1989), 254. See also 126–7.

[33] See Marcel Sarot, 'Religion, meaning and imitation. The Christian ideal of *imitatio Christi* as a way of making sense of life', in Marcel Sarot and Gijsbert van den Brink (eds), *Identity and Change in the Christian Tradition* (Frankfurt a/M, 1999).

CHAPTER 6

The Doctrine of the Trinity

Atonement and the Trinity

God's acts of atonement are Trinitarian in the sense that all three Persons of the Trinity are involved in reconciling us to God. This can best be explained in the light of the three freedoms that, according to St Bernard, God should grant us in order for us to be reconciled with him. As I explained in Chapter 3, these are *liberum arbitrium* (freedom of choice or freedom from necessity), *liberum consilium* (freedom of councel or freedom from sin) and *liberum complacitum* (freedom of pleasure or freedom from suffering).

It is our *liberum arbitrium* that makes us persons in relation to God. It is only through exercising this freedom that we can as persons be the free initiators of our own actions. As I argued in Chapter 2, this freedom is a necessary condition for us to enjoy the loving fellowship of God since such fellowship is a relation between persons. Like God we should also be free and autonomous agents in the relation. In this regard Bernard states that *liberum arbitrium* is the *image* of God in us. This means that God the Father has created us as the kind of beings who, like him, can enjoy loving fellowship. Such fellowship with God is the very purpose of our creation as human persons, the divine aim of human existence. Of course, this kind of freedom is *bestowed* on us by God. We do not owe our autonomy as persons to ourselves.

According to Bernard, we have not lost our *liberum arbitrium* as a result of the Fall. Thus the Father does not only create us as persons but he also sustains us as such in spite of the fact that we become estranged from him. Even in our state of estrangement we retain our status as persons in the image of God. By sustaining us as personal beings who may enjoy his loving fellowship, God keeps open the possibility for us to be reconciled with him.

By thus bestowing *liberum arbitrium* on us, God freely assumes the vulnerability of love in relation to us. In fact, he becomes even more vulnerable than we do since he cannot count on the steadfastness of our love in the way in which we can count on his steadfastness. Simone Weil explains this point as follows:

> God's creative love which maintains us in existence is not merely a superabundance of generosity, it is also renunciation and sacrifice. Not only the Passion but the Creation itself is a renunciation and sacrifice on the part of God. The Passion is simply its consummation. God already voids himself of his divinity by the Creation. He takes the form of a slave, submits to necessity, abases himself. His love maintains in existence, in a free and autonomous existence, beings other than himself, beings other than the good, mediocre beings. Through

love he abandons them to affliction and sin. If he did not abandon them they would not exist.[1]

Even if we were to express this point in less extreme terms than Simone Weil, it remains true that if God did not grant us the freedom and the ability to sin and cause affliction to him and to one another, we would not have the kind of free and autonomous existence necessary to enter as persons into loving fellowship with God and with one another. In the words of Sartre, 'if the beloved is transformed into an automaton, the lover finds himself alone'.[2] God is, of course, free to withhold this *liberum arbitrium* from us and turn us into automata. There is no necessity compelling God to create free persons beyond himself. It is God's own free and autonomous decision to create and sustain us as persons in order that we might enjoy his loving fellowship. In this sense God does not lose his own autonomy by granting us the gift of *liberum arbitrium*.

Clearly then, *liberum arbitrium* is a gift bestowed on us by God the Father who creates and sustains us as the kind of beings who can enjoy loving fellowship with him and with each other. As such this kind of freedom is also a necessary condition for us to be reconciled with God and to have our fellowship with him restored. However, *liberum arbitrium* is not enough. As I explained in Chapter 3, Bernard argues that we also require the other two freedoms, *liberum consilium* and *liberum complacitum*, in order to enjoy the loving fellowship of God. While *liberum arbitrium* is the *image* of God that we retain even in our state of estrangement, the other two freedoms are for Bernard the twofold *likeness* of God that we have lost by becoming estranged from God.

Liberum consilium is the freedom to know God and to consistently make his will our own and live our lives in accordance with it. In our state of estrangement we have become ignorant of God and of ourselves and have also become powerless by ourselves to live our lives in accordance with his will. Thus Bernard argues that we can only regain our lost *liberum consilium* if God were to grant us the gifts of enlightenment and empowerment. In the previous chapter I explained how the gift of enlightenment is granted to us in the incarnation of the Son. In the life and death of Jesus, God reveals himself to us and also makes his will known to us in order that we might make it our own. The gift of empowerment is again the work of the Father who creates for us the capacities and the opportunities to live our lives as icons of Christ.

Liberum complacitum is the freedom of pleasure by which we delight in living in the fellowship of God. We can regain this freedom, says Bernard, when God grants us the gift of 'wisdom' or 'taste' by which we may have a 'taste for the Good' and seek the will of God out of love and not merely out of duty. This is a gift of the Spirit of

---

[1] Simone Weil, *Gateway to God* (London, 1974), 80. For a Jewish view resembling that of Simone Weil, see Hans Jonas, 'The concept of God after Auschwitz', *The Journal of Religion*, 67 (1987), 1–13.

[2] Jean-Paul Sartre, *Being and Nothingness* (New York, 1956), 60. This obviously has far-reaching implications for the way in which we are to deal with the problem of evil and theodicy. I have discussed this point more extensively in Chapter 6 of my *Speaking of a Personal God* (Cambridge, 1992).

God who inspires us and fills our hearts with love and devotion for God. It is only through this gift of the Spirit that we are finally united with God in fellowship and can come to enjoy ultimate happiness.

The Spirit inspires our hearts but also illuminates our understanding. 'It is the Spirit that gives life' (John 6:63), but it is also the 'Spirit of truth' who will 'guide us into all the truth' (John 16:13). In this way we receive from the Spirit not only love but also faith. It is here that Calvin's definition of faith is helpful. According to him faith is 'a firm and sure knowledge of the divine favour towards us, founded on the truth of a free promise in Christ, and revealed to our minds, and sealed on our hearts, by the Holy Spirit'.[3] We will not be able to discern the 'divine favour' promised to us in Christ unless this is 'revealed to our minds and sealed on our hearts by the Holy Spirit': 'No one can say "Jesus is Lord" except under the influence of the Holy Spirit' (1 Corinthians 12:3). It is only with the eyes of faith that we can see Jesus as the Son of God in whom the forgiving love of God is revealed and as the Son of Man, the paradigm of human perfection in fellowship with God. Without the eyes of faith opened in us by the Spirit, we can see in Jesus no more than a first-century Jewish rabbi. At most he is a remarkable and charismatic human being but not the revelation of God. Divine revelation in Christ cannot be the object of historical or psychological research. In the words of Sir Edwyn Hoskyns: 'the glory of sonship ... cannot be observed by the historian or analysed by the psychologist. It is only accessible to those who believe.'[4] More generally we could say that discerning the agency of God in the world, whether creative, providential or revelatory, is not a matter of empirical perception. It is discernment with the 'eyes of faith' and as such something that the believer ascribes to the Holy Spirit.[5]

This has important implications for the way in which we are to understand the nature of religious experience. Such experience is often understood as in some way analogous to perception, but then as a special kind of extrasensory perception providing us with religious visions, voices, trances, revelations and the like. In this context the *via mystica* is often interpreted as a procedure for attaining such experiences. Frits Staal suggests that such experiences could also be achieved through 'the easy way of drugs' rather than 'the difficult ways of contemplation'. William James declares that 'I know more than one person who is persuaded that in the nitrous oxide trance we have a genuine metaphysical revelation.'[6] I think that this way of looking at religious experience is a *reductio ad absurdum* resulting from the misleading analogy with sense perception. Religious experience should not be

---

3   John Calvin, *Institutes of the Christian Religion*, 3.2.7, trans. Henry Beveridge (London, 1953).

4   Sir Edwyn Hoskyns, *The Fourth Gospel* (London 1947), vol. 1, 91. See also Maurice Wiles, *The Remaking of Christian Doctrine* (London, 1974), 48.

5   On discerning the acts of God, see chapter 5 of my *Speaking of a Personal God.*

6   William James, *Varieties of Religious Experience* (Glasgow, 1982), 373. See also Aldous Huxley, *The Doors of Perception* (London, 1954) for a classical defence of this claim. For Frits Staal's views, see his *Exploring Mysticism* (London, 1975). For a critical analysis of this view on mysticism, see chapter 3 of my *The Model of Love* (Cambridge, 1993).

interpreted as an extraordinary kind of extrasensory perception, but rather as ordinary experience (including ordinary sense perception) looked upon with the eyes of faith. In religious experience I understand my own life and actions, the sensory world in which I live and act, as well as events in the contemporary world and in history, in the light of my faith. In this way I experience my own life as a life of fellowship with God, the sensory world as an expression of the grace and glory of God, and events in the world as either realizations of God's intentions (and therefore good) or as contrary to the will of God (and therefore evil). So, too, I can look on events in history and in my own experience as providential or revelatory actions of God.

Let me illustrate this in the light of a classic example of religious experience, namely Isaiah's vision described in Isaiah 6:1–13. In the year that king Uzziah died, Isaiah participated in his official capacity as a prophet in some great religious festival (probably the annual enthronement feast) in the temple. Standing with the priests 'between the porch and the altar' (cf. Joel 2:17 and 2 Chronicles 20:4–19), he listened to the anthem of the temple ritual and gazed through the open portals of the sanctuary, now filled with the swirling smoke of incense, toward the innermost chamber where the Lord dwelt 'in thick darkness'. This ancient ceremony was rich in symbolism and familiar to all those present: 'To the worshipers it was a drama, familiar but still enthralling, that and nothing more. But to Isaiah, who had walked with God and grown ever more sensitive to spiritual and eternal values, suddenly there came an awareness of the divine reality behind the symbolism.'[7] In the light of his faith this scene gained a special significance for Isaiah. He heard the anthem of the temple ritual as if sung by seraphim around the throne of God, and the swirling smoke of incense in the sanctuary became for him the cloud of the Divine presence which according to Exodus 40:34 descended on the tabernacle in the desert. This filled him with a deep awareness of the holiness of God and of his own unworthiness in the Divine presence: 'Woe is me! I am doomed, for my own eyes have seen the King, the Lord of Hosts, I, a man of unclean lips, I, who dwell among a people of unclean lips' (Isaiah 6:5). This expression of his unworthiness before the holy God was followed by a profound awareness of divine forgiveness. It was as though 'one of the seraphim flew to me, carrying in his hand a glowing coal which he had taken from the altar with a pair of tongs. He touched my mouth with it and said: This has touched your lips; now your iniquity is removed and your sin is wiped out' (Isaiah 6:6–7). The experience of Divine forgiveness then evoked in Isaiah an awareness of his calling as a prophet: 'I heard the Lord saying: Whom shall I send? Who will go for us? I said: Here am I! Send me. He replied: Go, tell this people: However hard you listen, you will never understand. However hard you look, you will never perceive' (Isaiah 6:8–9).

Four things are clear from this example. First, religious experience is not a kind of extrasensory perception resulting from drugs or ascetic deprivation but, rather, a normal or at most an unusual experience understood in the light of faith. Secondly,

---

[7] G.G.D. Kilpatrick, *The Interpreters Bible*, vol. 5 (New York, 1956), 205.

this kind of understanding does not come naturally to us: 'However hard you listen, you will never understand. However hard you look, you will never perceive.' In the words of John Calvin,

> with regard to the knowledge of God, the knowledge of his paternal favour, which constitutes our salvation ... the most ingenious are blinder than moles ... Their discernment was not such as to direct them to the truth, far less to enable them to attain it, but resembles that of the bewildered traveller, who sees the flash of lightning glance far and wide for a moment, and then vanish into the darkness of the night, before he can advance a single step.[8]

I think that Calvin is rather optimistic here. Most of his travellers today are not even aware of the fact that they are bewildered! Even the flash of lightning remains hidden from them. Thirdly, for believers the Holy Spirit is held to be the primary agent of our spirituality and our religious experience. To quote Calvin again, 'it is when the Spirit, with a wondrous and special energy, forms the ear to hear and the mind to understand ... It thus appears that none can enter into the Kingdom of God save those whose minds have been renewed by the enlightenment of the Holy Spirit.'[9] It is thus through illumination by the Spirit that we are able to see all things with the eyes of faith. It is the Spirit that makes 'the penny drop'.[10] Finally, religious experience is transforming. It not only transforms the way we look at things but also our attitudes and actions in relation to them. Isaiah's vision transformed his life. In this way illumination of the understanding in the light of faith leads to inspiration of the heart and renewal of life in the fellowship of God. In this way the gifts of illumination and inspiration that we receive from the Spirit are closely connected.

In this section I have tried to show how God's activity in reconciling us with himself is Trinitarian in the sense that it involves the creativity of the Father, the revelation of the Son and the illumination and inspiration of the Spirit. How are these three forms of divine agency related? What is the relation between the three 'Persons' of the Trinity?

Social Trinitarianism

In the theological tradition a distinction has often been made between the 'economic Trinity' and the 'essential Trinity'. The former refers to the Trinitarian way in which God manifests himself in his dealings with us. It is this 'economic Trinity' that I have tried to explain in the previous section. The 'essential Trinity' refers to the 'inner life of the Godhead'. The question that arises here is whether and in what sense the Trinitarian way in which God deals with us (the economic Trinity) entails a Trinity in 'the inner life of the Godhead' (the essential Trinity). With this question we reach a point where we should tread very warily indeed. We know God in the way he deals with us and this

---

[8] John Calvin, *Institutes of the Christian Religion*, 2.2.18.

[9] John Calvin, *Institutes of the Christian Religion*, 2.2.20.

[10] Ian Ramsey, *Religious Language* (London, 1957), 19f.

knowledge is adequate to enable us to enjoy a life of fellowship with him. It is not for us to venture into speculations about the 'inner life of the Godhead'. Here we reach the point of mystery where God 'dwells in unapproachable light' (1 Timothy 6:16). Here it behoves us to remain agnostic and apophatic. Here we should desist from treating the mystery of faith as a mere puzzle of doctrine that we can sort out to our own satisfaction.

However, with this caveat in mind, the 'economic Trinity' does raise an important question which we cannot avoid asking. We have seen that God's dealings with us involve three forms of agency: creation, revelation and inspiration. The question is whether these three forms of agency also entail three distinct agents: the Father, the Son and the Spirit? Or are we to understand the Father, the Son and the Spirit as three ways in which one and the same divine Agent is manifested in his dealings with us? Both these views have had their supporters in the Christian tradition.

The standard way in which the Fathers described the relationship between the Father, the Son and the Spirit was to say that they are three Persons (*hypostases* or *personae*) in one Substance (*ousia* or *substantia*). The problem is that these terms are ambiguous with the result that the formula 'three Persons in one Substance' allows for more than one interpretation. Thus, Aristotle distinguishes between two uses of the term *ousia* or substance.[11] On the one hand he speaks of a 'primary substance' in the sense of a discrete individual entity that has properties and stands in relations to other such primary substances. It is not itself a property or relation of something else. What Aristotle calls a 'secondary substance' is the essential property or nature that makes a thing to be the thing it is. Thus, individual trees are primary substances whereas the essential property or nature of 'treeness' that they share and that makes them the things they are (that is, trees), is a secondary substance. This means that the meaning of the formula 'three Persons in one Substance' is different depending on whether it refers to one primary or one secondary substance.

In general the Latin Fathers favoured the view that the 'one Substance' in the formula refers to a primary substance. The triune God was a single discrete individual entity. In this they subscribed to the monotheism of the biblical tradition. The Law tells us to 'hear, o Israel: the Lord our God is one' (Deuteronomy 6:4) and Jesus tells us that he came not to destroy the Law but to perfect or fulfil it (Matthew 5:17) and, according to Mark 12:29, he specifically endorsed the *shema*. I think that Brian Leftow expresses the attitude of the Latin Fathers well by saying that this 'lays down a condition Christian theology must meet: the Christian version of monotheism should complete, perfect or fulfil its Jewish version. It should be monotheism a Jew could accept as monotheistic, and a completion of Jewish monotheism.'[12] Hence, for the Latin Fathers there can be only one God in the strong sense of a single individual primary substance.

This raised for them the problem of what to do with the 'three Persons' in the Trinitarian formula. It is obvious that they cannot also be primary substances or

---

[11] On this point see William P. Alston, 'Substance and the Trinity', in Stephen T. Davis, Daniel Kendall and Gerald O'Collins (eds), *The Trinity* (Oxford, 1999).

[12] Brian Leftow, 'Anti social Trinitarianism', in Stephen T. Davis, Daniel Kendall and Gerald O'Collins (eds), *The Trinity* (Oxford, 1999), 235–6.

discrete individual entities. The 'Persons' in the formula can therefore not be taken as persons in the sense that we understand this term today. For the Latin Fathers they were therefore taken to be secondary substances, that is, in some sense or other essential properties or relations of the one Divine primary substance. The 'Persons' were *distinct* properties or relations but not *discrete* entities. In this way the Latin Fathers fulfilled the injunction in the Athanasian Creed that they should 'neither confound the Persons nor divide the Substance'. This approach to the doctrine of the Trinity can be called *Latin Trinitarianism*. I will discuss this type of Trinitarianism in the next section.

A different approach was generally defended in the Eastern Church, and more specifically by the Cappadocian Fathers in the late fourth century: Basil the Great, Gregory of Nazianzus and Gregory of Nyssa. For them the triune God consists of three 'Persons' (taken to be discrete individual entities or primary substances) who share the one essential property or nature (secondary substance) of divinity. Thus Basil explains the unity of the Persons in the divine essence or nature by comparing it with four individuals named Peter, Andrew, John and James, who are all one in that they belong to the species 'man'. They were all primary substances who shared the same essential human nature (secondary substance). In this sense the 'Persons' in the Trinity were not only *distinct* but also *discrete*. Nevertheless they were also one in the sense that they shared the *same* divine nature. The Cappadocians could therefore also claim that they neither 'confused the Persons' nor 'divided the substance'. This approach is often referred to as *social Trinitarianism* since it tends to view the Trinity as in some sense or other a 'society' or 'community' consisting of three individual divine entities.

The obvious difficulty with this approach is that it seems to deviate from the monotheism of the biblical tradition. To claim that the Trinity consists of three discrete divine beings looks more like tritheism than like monotheism. The fact that the three Persons share the same divine nature does not make them one God any more than the Olympian gods can be called 'one god' because they share the essential property of being gods!

In the case of the Cappadocians, the matter is more complicated. We should not forget that they were Platonists and, as I have shown at length in previous chapters, their Platonism entailed that for them the universal was more real than the particular. For Platonists, essential natures (the Aristotelian secondary substances) are much more real than particular entities (Aristotelian primary substances) which participate in them or manifest them. 'Treeness' is much more real than individual trees. Thus the universal divine Nature was much more real that the three particular 'Persons' who participate in it or in whom it is manifested.[13] In this way the three divine Persons are

---

[13] On this point see Maurice Wiles, *The Making of Christian Doctrine* (Cambridge, 1967), 132f. 'For them as thoroughgoing Platonists the *ousia* that is common to all men is not an abstract concept but the most real thing that there is. It is this fact, so foreign to our way of thought, that is determinative of their understanding of the divine *ousia* and which shows them to be essentially monotheistic in intention. Their use of *ousia*, therefore, must be understood within the setting of a radical Platonism ... Within a fully Platonist framework any individual concretion of *ousia* must necessarily have a lesser degree of reality than the *ousia* itself' (ibid., 133).

no more than particular manifestations or concretions of the one essential divine Nature that is God. Understood in this way, the Cappadocian view of the Trinity is not so far removed from Latin Trinitarianism.[14]

If, as Wiles correctly points out, such Platonist ways of thinking are 'so foreign to our way of thought', this Platonist argument used by the Cappadocians, is no longer available to present-day social Trinitarians when defending themselves against the charge of tritheism. The question is therefore whether such present-day social Trinitarians can still claim to be monotheists if they are to abandon the Platonist assumptions of the Cappadocians. Some contemporary social Trinitarians simply abandon the claim to be monotheists. In this way Jürgen Moltmann *criticizes* Karl Barth's Latin views on the Trinity for being a form of 'Christian monotheism'.[15] Others, like Richard Swinburne, take leave of this claim implicity by discussing the Trinity in terms of three Gods.[16]

Most contemporary social Trinitarians try to show that their social Trinitarianism can still be called monotheist. They usually do so by emphasizing the unity between the Persons of the Trinity and developing the disanalogy between the way in which the Persons of the Trinity are related to each other and the way in which human persons are. Here they also make use of the ways in which the Cappadocians set limits to Basil's analogy between the three Persons of the Trinity, on the one hand, and 'Peter, Andrew, John and James', on the other.

A good example of a contemporary social Trinitarian is Cornelius Plantinga. According to him a social theory of the Trinity

> must have Father, Son, and Spirit as distinct centres of knowledge, will, love, and action. Since each of these capacities require consciousness, it follows that, on this sort of theory, Father, Son, and Spirit would be viewed as distinct centres of consciousness or, in short, as *persons* in some full sense of the term.

Furthermore,

> Father, Son, and Spirit must be regarded as tightly enough related to each other so as to render plausible the judgement that they constitute a particular social unit. In such social monotheism, it will be appropriate to use the designator *God* for the whole Trinity, where the Trinity is understood to be one thing, even if it is a complex thing consisting of persons, essences, and relations.[17]

---

[14] In an interesting essay Sarah Coakley argues that Gregory of Nyssa's views on the Trinity can 'rather more easily shelter under' what is called 'Latin Trinitarianism' than under what is called 'social Trinitarianism'. See Sarah Coakley, 'Persons in the social doctrine of the Trinity: a critique of current analytic discussion', in Stephen T. Davis, Daniel Kendall and Gerald O'Collins (eds), *The Trinity* (Oxford, 1999), 137.

[15] Jürgen Moltmann, *The Trinity and the Kingdom of God* (London, 1981), 139–44.

[16] For example: 'There is overriding reason for the first God to create a second God and with him to create a third God.' Richard Swinburne, 'Could there be more than one God?', *Faith and Philosophy*, 5 (1988), 233. In his more recent book *The Christian God* (Oxford, 1994), 177, Swinburne repeats this argument but now talks of 'divine individuals' rather than of 'Gods'.

[17] Cornelius Plantinga Jr, 'Social Trinity and tritheism', in Ronald J. Feenstra and Cornelius Plantinga Jr. (eds), *Trinity, Incarnation, and Atonenent* (Notre Dame, IN, 1989), 22.

The plausibility of the claim that this view can count as monotheism, depends on whether the connection between the three persons can be made tight enough to justify the claim that 'the Trinity is understood to be one thing'. On the other hand, the connection cannot be made so tight as to jeopardize the separate reality of the Persons. For this reason Plantinga rejects the traditional Platonist doctrine of divine simplicity in which Father, Son and Spirit 'are said to be identical with the divine essence, thus making the *de facto* number of persons in God hard to estimate'.[18] This entails a rejection of the Platonism in terms of which the Cappadocian Fathers understood the unity of the Godhead since for Plantinga that fails to do sufficient justice to the separate reality of the Persons. The problem for the defenders of such 'social monotheism' is on the one hand to make the connection between the Persons tight enough to guarantee the unity of the Godhead and therefore still to count as monotheism, and on the other hand not to make the connection so tight as to jeopardize the separate reality of the Persons who make up the 'particular social unit' that is God.

There are a number of ways in which contemporary social Trinitarians interpret the relationship between the Persons of the Trinity in order to uphold the claim of monotheism. Thus social Trinitarians often interpret the inner-Trinitarian relation as one of perfect love between the Father, the Son and the Spirit. For this view they appeal to St Augustine who held that the relation between the Father and the Son is one of perfect love and that the Spirit is the bond of love that binds them together. The trouble with this view is that it seems to depersonalize the Spirit. The Spirit becomes a relation between the Father and the Son rather than a third Person in the divine triad. In the twelfth century Richard of St Victor held that the loving relation should be extended to include the Spirit as a third party. He argued that love, to be perfect, must be shared by a third person. In God we find not merely an I-thou relation of mutual love between the Father and the Son but it also includes the Holy Spirit as co-beloved (*condilectus*). A contemporary social Trinitarian like Richard Swinburne develops this view further. He argues that

> love is a supreme good. Love involves sharing, giving to the other what of one's own is good for him and receiving from the other what of his is good for one; and love involves co-operating with another to benefit third parties. The latter is crucial to worthwhile love. There would be something deeply unsatisfactory (even if for inadequate humans sometimes unavoidable) about a marriage in which the parties were concerned solely with each other and did not use their mutual love to bring forth good for others ... Love must share and love must co-operate in sharing ... A divine individual would see that for him too a best kind of action would be to share and to co-operate in sharing.[19]

On these grounds Swinburne argues that a loving God should necessarily consist of a Trinity of 'divine individuals' bound together by a bond of loving co-operation. The

---

[18] Plantinga, 'Social Trinity and tritheism', 22.

[19] Swinburne, *The Christian God*, 177–8.

unity between the three Persons in the Trinity consists therefore in the bond of mutual love and co-operation.

Is this unity sufficient to justify the claim that such a view is monotheistic? In Chapter 2 I argued that love, both human and divine, is a relationship between persons who are autonomous agents in relation to each other and freely identify with each other. Their love is in no way necessitated but springs from the free choice of each partner. If this is the relation between the Persons of the Trinity, then it follows that they are separate autonomous individual agents in relation to each other, 'divine individuals' as Swinburne calls them. This is hardly enough to justify the claim that together they are 'one God'. Of course, the bond of love that ties them together distinguishes them from the Olympian gods, 'divine individuals' who are continually squabbling with each other. If, however, the Olympic gods were to be more co-operative and better behaved, that would not yet justify calling belief in them monotheistic.[20]

Maybe 'love' has its limitations as a metaphor for inner-Trinitarian relations. The relation between the Persons of the Trinity is too different from human relations, and even from the divine–human bond of love to which believers aspire, to be described as 'love' in such an unqualified sense. Here St Bernard distinguishes the *unity* between the Persons of the Trinity from the kind of *union* which a believer seeks with God:

> There is in them [the Father and the Son] ... but one essence and one will, and where there is only one, there can be no agreement or combining or incorporation or anything of that kind. For there must be at least two wills for there to be agreement, and two essences for there to be combining and uniting in agreement. There is none of these things in the Father and the Son since they have neither two essences nor two wills ... If anyone would affirm that there is agreement between the Father and the Son, I do not contest it provided that it is understood that there is not a union of wills but a unity of will. But we think of God and man as dwelling in each other in a very different way, because their wills and their substances are distinct and different; that is, their substances are not intermingled, yet their wills are in agreement; and this union is for them a communion of wills and an agreement in charity. Happy is this union if you experience it, but compared with the other, it is no union at all.[21]

Social Trinitarians like Swinburne who describe the relations within the Trinity in terms of the metaphor of love, think of these relations as 'a communion of wills and an agreement in charity' with the result that they do not constitute a *unity* as is required in monotheism but merely the kind of *union* which believers aspire to attain with God. The Trinitarian Persons remain separate 'divine individuals' each with its own will, mind, essence, and so on. In the words of Plantinga quoted above, they are 'distinct centres of knowledge, will, love, and action' as well as 'distinct centres of consciousness'. This is hardly sufficient to counter the charge of tritheism.

---

[20] On this point see Leftow, 'Anti social trinitarianism', 232–3.

[21] St Bernard, *Sermons on the Song of Songs,* 4 vols (Kalamazoo, MI, 1971–80), sermon 71.

Brian Hebblethwaite, who is sympathetic to the social model of the Trinity, tries to avoid its tritheisic implications by stressing that 'the social analogy is an *analogy* ...[that] has to be qualified precisely at the point where the spectre of tritheism looms'.[22] This point is where human personal relations are *external*: 'We must not allow the human side of the analogy to dominate our grasp of the divine side. If human persons exist in relation only externally, over against other individuals, this is precisely *not* the feature to be extrapolated into God.'[23] According to Hebblethwaite the relations within the Trinity are *internal* relations:

> God himself, in his own being, exists in an internal relationship of love given and love received. That love ... was mirrored in the relationship between Jesus and the Father. That same love [believers] experience in their own lives ... as a relationship in which they too [are] caught up and could come to share ... The very notion of a God who is love requires us to think of an internally differentiated and relational deity.[24]

The mistake with tritheism is that it views the Trinity as 'a number of finite supernatural beings related externally, each existing in a sphere exclusive of the other or others'.[25]

I fear that Hebblethwaite's solution faces some serious difficulties. As I have argued in Chapter 2, persons are by definition autonomous agents who freely initiate their own actions. *Liberum arbitrium* belongs to our nature as persons. It follows that personal relations like loving fellowship are by definition *external* relations since they lack the necessity that belongs to internal relations. Persons logically cannot be internally related. Love can only be freely given and freely received, otherwise it is not love at all. It is therefore a contradiction in terms to speak of 'an internal relationship of love given and love received'. Of course, God is not like other people since his goodness, power and knowledge are unlimited. It follows that concepts like 'personhood' and 'love' can only be applied in a qualified sense to God and to his relationship with us.[26] If, however, we are also to apply the analogy to the internal relations within the Trinity, we will have to qualify it further to the point of equivocation. Furthermore, it makes no sense to claim that the internal relations within the Trinity are relations in which we are 'caught up and could come to share'. This can only be done within a unitive mysticism where the human is somehow merged into the divine. Hebblethwaite himself quite correctly rejects this option.[27] The analogy can indeed be applied to the loving fellowship that Jesus displayed

---

[22] Brian Hebblethwaite, *The Incarnation. Collected Essays in Christology* (Cambridge, 1987), 20.

[23] Hebblethwaite, *The Incarnation*, 135.

[24] Hebblethwaite, *The Incarnation*, 21–2. See also 64.

[25] Hebblethwaite, *The Incarnation*, 20.

[26] See Chapter 2 above. I have analysed these qualifications in more detail in chapter 9 of my *The Model of Love*.

[27] 'Once we start speaking of ourselves in any sense as *being* God, we have lost touch with Christianity' (Hebblethwaite, *The Incarnation*, 18). For a critical analysis of this kind of mysticism, see chapter 3 of my *The Model of Love*.

towards the Father, since this reveals to us the perfect fellowship with God on which God desires us to pattern our lives. But then, as I have argued in the previous chapter, the fellowship that Jesus displays towards the Father manifests his perfect humanity rather than his divinity. The prayers of Jesus to the Father do not make known to us 'his inner-Trinitarian relations ... to the Father',[28] but rather the perfect divine–human relationship that we are called upon to emulate in our lives. The way that Jesus relates to the Father is the perfect manifestation of what St Bernard calls the *union* of love and not of the *unity* within the Trinity.

Apart from the metaphor of love, there are two other considerations by means of which contemporary social Trinitarians try to tighten the relation between the persons of the Trinity, and which they derive from the Cappadocians: the doctrine of perichoresis and its corollary, the doctrine of the unity of operations of the Trinity (*opera Trinitatis ad extra sunt indivisa*). *Perichoresis* is the Greek word for 'encircling' or 'encompassing' and was used by the Cappadocians in the technical sense of 'mutual interpenetration' to refer to the co-inherence of the three persons in the one eternal God. This idea only makes sense in the light of the Platonist assumptions of the Cappadocians. The divine Persons are one in being because they are three particular concretions of the one universal divine *ousia*. This unity of being shows itself in the unity of operations. This is where the Trinity differs from Basil's 'Peter, Andrew, John and James', distinct human persons whose actions can be ascribed to distinct personal agents. In the words of Gregory of Nyssa, 'in the case of the Divine nature, we do not [as in the case of men] learn that the Father does anything by himself in which the Son does not work conjointly, and again that the Son has any special operation apart from the Holy Spirit'.[29] In other words, the operations of the persons of the Trinity are not ascribed to separate agents but they all issue from the one universal divine *ousia* that is God. Here again the Cappadocian view seems to me more 'Latin' than 'social'!

If, however, we were to take leave of the Platonism of the Cappadocians, this view becomes unintelligible. Thus Cornelius Plantinga describes the doctrine of perichoresis as 'a sort of intratrinitarian hospitality concept. According to this concept, each Trinitarian person graciously makes room for the others in his own inner life and envelops or enfolds that person there. Each is *in* the other two.'[30] I must confess that I have no idea what this could mean. I can sympathize with Dale Tuggy's bafflement with this concept of perichoresis.[31]

The doctrine of the unity of divine operations raises serious epistemological difficulties for social Trinitarians. As Maurice Wiles points out,

> if there is no distinction whatever in the activity of the Trinity towards us, how can we have any knowledge of the distinctions at all? It is logically impossible ...

---

[28] Hebblethwaite, *The Incarnation*, 24.

[29] Gregory, *Ad Graecos*, 24–5. Quoted by Coakley, 'Persons in the social doctrine of the Trinity', 132.

[30] Plantinga, 'Social Trinity and tritheism', 25.

[31] Dale Tuggy, 'The unfinished business of Trinitarian theorizing', *Religious Studies*, 39 (2003), 170–71.

to claim that they are known to us as a result of rational reflection on those particular manifestations of the divine activity which centre in the birth, ministry, crucifixion, resurrection and ascension of Jesus Christ and the gift of the Holy Spirit to the Church.[32]

For the Cappadocians the only difference between the Persons of the Trinity is located in their internal relations to one another: the Son is 'begotten' or 'generated' by the Father and the Spirit 'proceeds' from the Father and the Son. This does not help us much, however, since

> not only is there no difference in the operations, through which we might come to know of the different persons of the Trinity, but we are not even given any idea of the difference in the meaning between the relationships of 'generation' and 'procession' – the only difference which is admitted to exist.[33]

In the end the Cappadocians prefer to remain apophatic about the inner working of the divine *ousia*.[34] I think that is as it should be.

The best that contemporary social Trinitarians can make of these doctrines is Swinburne's idea of loving co-operation between the persons of the Trinity. Perichoresis then becomes the loving bond of concurrence and mutual accord between them, and the unity of their operations consists in the fact that their actions are always co-operative operations in which they jointly participate. In this way the persons of the Trinity remain separate 'divine individuals' (as Swinburne calls them) and the *union* of love that binds them together does not constitute the *unity* required by monotheism.

Clearly, then, contemporary social Trinitarians are faced with an insoluble dilemma: either they interpret the inner-Trinitarian relation as a union of love, in which case they cannot avoid the charge of tritheism, or they interpret it as an internal relation of unity, in which case they can no longer maintain the claim that the Trinitarian Persons are discrete 'divine individuals' who together form a social community. What Plantinga calls 'social monotheism' can be social or it can be monotheism, but it cannot be both.

Looking on God as a 'particular social unit' (Plantinga) is also unsatisfactory from the point of view of the claim that ultimate happiness consists in enjoying the loving fellowship of God. As I have argued in Chapter 2, loving fellowship is a relationship between two personal beings in the sense of individual free agents. If God is a community of persons, it becomes incoherent to talk of loving fellowship with God, since a community of persons is not itself a personal agent, no matter how closely the persons co-operate in their actions. Leftow makes a similar point with reference to Swinburne: 'one who worships addresses someone. So worship makes sense only if directed to someone who can be aware of being addressed. Collections are not

---

32 Maurice Wiles, *Working Papers in Doctrine* (London, 1976), 14.

33 Wiles, *Working Papers in Doctrine*, 14.

34 See Coakley, 'Persons in the social doctrine of the Trinity, 135–6.

conscious … So one cannot appropriately worship Swinburne's collective.'[35] And again:

> those who use 'God' to address a prayer to its hearer err as one would who addresses the holders of a joint Presidency as 'Mr. President' … So too, the voice from the burning bush should have introduced itself as 'We are', not 'I am' – or else we should enquire which of the Three spoke there, or conclude that the 'I' of 'I am' is ambiguous.[36]

In this connection it is significant to note with John Burnaby that 'the main Christian tradition … has instinctively avoided speaking of the Trinity by the plural pronoun "they", even when a plural verb was inevitable. The original Latin text of the Athanasian Creed manages very skilfully to avoid the use even of a plural verb!'[37]

It is clear that social Trinitarianism faces formidable difficulties in trying to accommodate the monotheism of biblical faith and the spirituality of loving fellowship with God. Furthermore, in the end such speculative constructions regarding the 'inner life of the Godhead' transcend the bounds of what we can know and intrudes into the sphere of mystery where we should remain apophatic. Maybe we should be satisfied to limit ourselves to the 'economic Trinity' and desist from speculative claims about the 'essential Trinity'. Maybe Wiles is right in arguing that

> to speak of a knowledge of God in himself, abstracted from our apprehension of him in a relationship of faith and adoration, suggests a detached, spectator attitude, a knowledge of the head rather than of the heart. Even if such a knowledge were possible philosophically, would it not be regarded as religiously arid and arrogant? To know Christ is to know his benefits. To limit our knowledge of God to knowledge of his effects as experienced should not … be seen as an abdication of any vital religious concern, but rather as the safeguarding of a genuine religious form of knowledge against the pride of human self-assertion.[38]

Maybe we should conclude that the Trinitarian nature of God's acts of atonement does not justify the claim that the Trinity consists of three separate agents or 'divine individuals'. In fact the claim that the *opera Trinitatis ad extra sunt indivisa*, to which some social Trinitarians subscribe, itself excludes the possibility of such an inference. Should we not go rather for the claim of Latin Trinitarianism that the *opera Trinitatis* all issue from one and the same divine Agent who is God?

Latin Trinitarianism

Latin Trinitarians look on God as a single personal being, the one and only focus of worship to whom all our prayers are addressed. In Aristotelian terms, God is a

---

[35] Leftow, 'Anti social Trinitarianism', 228.

[36] Leftow, 'Anti social Trinitarianism', 230.

[37] John Burnaby, *The Belief of Christendom. A Commentary on the Nicene Creed* (London, 1959), 210.

[38] Wiles, *The Remaking of Christian Doctrine*, 26.

'primary substance'. This does not mean that we do not worship the Father and the Son and the Holy Spirit. In doing so, however, we do not worship three separate 'divine individuals' but one and the same personal God who relates to us as Father, Son and Spirit. In the words of Karl Barth,

> it follows from the trinitarian understanding of the God revealed in Scripture, that this one God is to be understood not just as impersonal lordship, i.e., as power, but as the Lord, not just as absolute Spirit but as person, i.e., as an I existing in and for itself with its own thought and will. This is how he meets us in his revelation. This is how he is thrice God as Father, Son and Spirit.[39]

Even though God is in many ways not like other people, he is nevertheless a 'person' like us in the sense of the kind of individual being with whom we can enjoy loving fellowship. The Father, the Son and the Spirit are not considered to be separate individual 'persons' in the way maintained by social Trinitarians.

In what sense then can Latin Trinitarians still speak of the Father, the Son and the Spirit as 'Persons'? Here John Burnaby points out that

> we have to remind ourselves that the word "Person" itself, indispensable as it is in our discourse about the Three-in-Oneness of God, is a technical term ... *Hypostasis* is not equivalent to our word 'person', for it does not of itself connote a thinking and acting individual: not every *hypostasis* is a person, though every person is a *hypostasis*. The Latin *persona*, on the other hand, is more specific in meaning than *hypostasis*, and in ordinary use is only applicable to human beings; but it denotes the individual, not as the bearer of 'personality' in our sense of the word, but in his relation to society, as the bearer of rights and functions. So neither the Greek nor the Latin word carried with it when applied to the divine Trinity the implication of an individual centre of conscious life and independent agency.[40]

In the previous section I argued that in Latin Trinitarianism Father, Son and Holy Spirit are viewed as 'secondary substances', that is, in some sense as essential 'properties' or 'relations' of the one primary substance, God. Thus St Augustine recognizes that the Three are traditionally designated as Persons but is clearly unhappy about the term because it conveyed the suggestion of separate individuals to him. He went to great lengths to argue that they cannot be three persons in the sense in which Abraham, Isaac and Jacob were three persons. In the end he consents to adopt the current usage 'not because that is what we wanted to say, but so as not to be reduced to silence'.[41] More positively, Augustine tried to explain the three Persons in one God in the light of psychological analogies in the human soul. These were for him 'vestiges' of God expressing the image of God in us. For him the most satisfactory analogy was that of memory, understanding and will. These do not exist

---

[39] Karl Barth, *The Doctrine of the Word of God* (*Church Dogmatics* I.1) (Edinburgh, 1975), 358–9.

[40] Burnaby, *The Belief of Christendom*, 202–203. On the different meanings of the term 'person' see also Jenny Teichman, 'The definition of *person*', *Philosophy*, 60 (1985), 175–85.

[41] St Augustine, *De Trinitate*, V.10, VII.11.

as three separable members of an organism but subsist as three ways in which the mind acts in relation to itself. Although Anselm, Aquinas and Calvin were not equally convinced by Augustine's psychological analogies, they followed him in arguing that the Three do not exist as separate individuals but all subsist in God.[42] For Karl Barth 'the triunity of God does not mean threefold deity either in the sense of a plurality of Gods or in the sense of the existence of a plurality of individuals or parts within the one Godhead'.[43] Since this is what is suggested by talk of 'three Persons', Barth prefers not to

> use the term 'person' but rather 'mode (or way) of being', our intention being to express by this term … more simply and clearly the same thing as is meant by 'person' … The statement that God is One in three ways of being, Father, Son and Holy Spirit, means, therefore, that the one God, i.e. the one Lord, the one personal God, is what he is not just in one mode but … in the mode of the Father, in the mode of the Son, and in the mode of the Holy Spirit.[44]

In the first paragraph of this chapter, I suggested that we understand the 'Persons' of the Trinity in terms of the Trinitarian structure of God's acts of atonement. Rather than Barth's 'modes of being' or Rahner's 'modes of subsistence' I prefer, therefore, to talk of 'modes of agency'. This point is well stated by Christoph Schwöbel who argues that

> the trinitarian perspective makes it possible to distinguish creation, revelation and inspiration as three basic types of action which constitute divine agency without making it necessary to posit three different agents … Talking of the agency of God the Father, The Son and the Spirit within the terms I have outlined would enable us to insist that there is only one *agent*, whilst allowing that there are three distinctive though internally related *types of action* … This analysis of the trinitarian structure of Christian belief in God seems to avoid the danger of tritheism or of conceiving God as some kind of tripartite being.[45]

Understanding the 'Persons' as modes or types of action connects up well with the Latin *persona* used to refer to the theatrical 'masks' which represent the various *dramatis personae* or roles played by actors.[46] The one divine Actor fulfils three roles in his dealing with us humans.

There are especially two serious objections that contemporary social Trinitarians often raise against all such Latin forms of Trinitarianism. The first objection is that

---

[42] See Barth, *The Doctrine of the Word of God*, 355–8. Following Aquinas, Karl Rahner refers to the Three as 'three distinct forms of subsistence' (Rahner, *The Trinity* [New York, 1970]).

[43] Barth, *The Doctrine of the Word of God*, 350.

[44] Barth, *The Doctrine of the Word of God*, 359.

[45] Christoph Schwöbel, 'Divine agency and providence', *Modern Theology*, 3 (1987), 240. Contrary to what he writes here, Schwöbel seems in his more recent writings to have become more sympathetic to the social model of the Trinity. See for example his *Gott in Beziehung* (Tübingen, 2002) and 'God is liefde: Het model van de liefde en de Triniteit', in L.J. van den Brom (ed.), *De Liefde Bevraagd* (Kampen, 1997).

[46] See J.N.L. Kelly, *Early Christian Doctrines* (London, 1977), 114–5.

Latin Trinitarianism is often dismissed as a form of modalism, a Western heresy in the early third century.[47] Although modalism can indeed be looked upon as a form of Latin Trinitarianism, it does not follow that all Latin Trinitarianism can count as modalist. It is not easy to reconstruct what modalism was exactly, since all the writings of modalists, like Noetus, Praxeas and Sabellius, were destroyed by their opponents. What remains for us is the attempts of scholars to piece together some sense of what the modalists said from allusions, quotations and (biased) reports which survive in the anti-modalist writings of their opponents.[48] The main objections against modalism can usefully be described as resulting from the fact that the modalists failed to take note of the limitations of the metaphor of theatre masks (*personae*) when this is used to explain the difference between the Trinitarian 'Persons'.[49] Three aspects of the metaphor are relevant here. First, a theatre mask is something behind which an actor is hidden. In their daily lives actors differ from the roles they play on stage and their true personality is not necessarily revealed in these roles. Secondly, these roles are fulfilled only briefly on stage. After playing the role the actor takes off the mask. Thirdly, the same actor can play various roles at various times and these roles could also exclude each other so that they cannot be fulfilled together. At these points the analogy does not carry over to Trinitarian theology.

First, the creating and sustaining Father, the revealing Son and the inspiring Spirit are not masks behind which God hides his true self from us but rather 'three basic types of action' in which he manifests his true self in relation to us. Thus Karl Barth points out that for the modalists the Trinitarian 'persons' are

> only manifestations behind which God's true being is concealed as something other and higher, so that one may ask whether revelation can be believed if in the background there is always the thought that we are not dealing with God as he is but only as he appears to us.[50]

God is *really* the Creator, Revealer and Inspirer as he manifests himself in his dealings with us. The essential Trinity is not something different from the economic Trinity: 'The revelation of God and therefore his being as Father, Son and Spirit is not an economy which is foreign to his essence ... so that we have to ask about a hidden Fourth if we are really to ask about God.'[51] Thus we really know God as he essentially is to the extent that he reveals himself in the economy of his threefold dealing with us. Of course, this does not deny the fact that there is much more to God in himself than he reveals to us. The 'inner life of the Godhead' remains a mystery that transcends the knowledge of him that we can derive from the economy of his actions in relation to

---

[47] On this point see for example Denis W. Jowels, 'The reproach of modalism: a difficulty for Karl Barth's doctrine of the Trinity', *Scottish Journal of Theology*, 56 (2003), 231–46.

[48] See for example Kelly, *Early Christian Doctrines*, ch. 5.

[49] According to Kelly this metaphor was originally used by Tertullian and Hippolytus rather than by the modalists whom they opposed (Kelly, *Early Christian Doctrines*, 115, 122). Nevertheless, it is still useful to explain the difficulties with modalism in terms of it.

[50] Barth, *The Doctrine of the Word of God*, 353.

[51] Barth, *The Doctrine of the Word of God*, 382.

us. However, what he reveals of himself is sufficient to enable us to live in his fellowship. We should be satisfied with that and desist from speculative probing into his essential 'inner life' beyond what he has revealed to us.

Secondly, the creating and sustaining Father, the revealing Son and the inspiring Spirit are not temporary and passing roles which God could abandon at any moment, but divine saving acts on which we can always depend for our eternal happiness. We can depend on God never to stop sustaining us, making himself known to us and inspiring us. It is in accordance with his divine character to do so and we can count on him to always remain faithful to his character. God is immutable in the *personal* sense of being faithful to his character and not in the *impersonal* sense of being absolutely unchanging and unable to accommodate himself adequately to our ever-changing needs and circumstances.[52]

Finally, creation, revelation and inspiration are not incompatible roles but essentially interconnected types of divine action: 'Just as without creation there is no revelation, and without revelation no inspiration, so without inspiration there is no awareness of revelation, and without this no awareness of creation. Hence creation, revelation and inspiration neither merely coexist nor coincide in an undifferentiated way.'[53] In this way we can make some sense of the doctrine of perichoresis, not as a doctrine about three divine agents who are intertwined with each other in some incomprehensible fashion, but as the doctrine of three interconnected forms of action performed by one and the same divine Agent: *opera Trinitatis ad extra sunt indivisa.* This interconnection of the divine acts also excludes the modalist idea that Father, Son and Spirit are roles that God fulfils consecutively. That would mean that when at the incarnation he takes on the role of the Son, he stops fulfilling the role of Creator and Sustainer of the universe and that it is only after Pentecost that he starts inspiring us! On the contrary, Father, Son and Spirit are all eternal in the sense that God is eternally the Creator, Revealer and Inspirer on whose loving agency we can depend for our eternal happiness in the fellowship we may enjoy with him.

It is clear that serious objections can be raised against third-century modalism as this was handed down to us and that the Fathers were right in rejecting it as a heresy. It is equally clear, however, that these objections do not apply to all forms of Latin Trinitarianism. There is therefore no reason to dismiss all Latin Trinitarianism as modalist.

The second serious objection that social Trinitarians often raise against Latin Trinitarianism is that it cannot account adequately for the claim that 'God is love' (1 John 4:8). C.F.J. Williams states this objection as follows:

> if love is God's nature, his love must have an object other than his creation, or any part of it: to believe otherwise would be to make God dependent for his innermost

---

[52] On this concept of divine immutability see my *What Are We Doing When We Pray?* (London, 1984), 34–40.

[53] Ingolf U. Dalferth, 'The eschatological roots of the doctrine of the Trinity', in Christoph Schwöbel (ed.), *Trinitarian Theology Today* (Edinburgh, 1995), 161.

activity on something that is not himself. But love is relational, and the relation in question is irreflexive: that is to say, it makes no sense to talk of a person loving herself ... Real love, love in the literal sense, requires more than one person. So if God is love, that love must involve the love of one person by another. And if creatures cannot be the only ones who are the objects of God's love, there must be a plurality of persons in the Godhead.[54]

In other words, if God is love and if love is a relationship then, either the Godhead must consist of three divine Persons tied together by an eternal bond of love, as social Trinitarians claim, or God is dependent on finite created persons to whom he can relate in a bond of love, as Latin Trinitarians claim. In that case God is not only dependent on finite creatures but also his love cannot be eternal since it can only come into being after he has created finite persons to love.

Brian Hebblethwaite expands this objection as follows:

there can be no doubt that the model of a single individual person does create difficulties for theistic belief. It presents us with the picture of one who, despite his infinite attributes, is unable to enjoy the excellence of personal relations unless he first create an object for his love. Monotheistic faiths have not favoured the idea that creation is necessary to God, but short of postulating personal relations in God, it is difficult to see how they can avoid it.[55]

Thus if God were to be a single individual and not three persons in relation, he would be dependent on the creation of persons beyond himself in order not only to enjoy the 'excellence of personal relations' but also 'to enjoy the fullness of being as love',[56] and even 'for being personal at all'.[57]

How can Latin Trinitarians deal with this objection? If, on the one hand, persons are autonomous agents who freely initiate their own action, then God cannot be said to be dependent on persons beyond himself 'for being personal at all'. God remains the kind of personal being with whom we can enjoy personal fellowship, even when we fail to enter into such fellowship with him and even if we were not to exist as beings with whom he can have such fellowship. On the other hand, if personal relations (including loving fellowship) are only possible between persons who are autonomous agents, then personal relations are by definition external relations between independent personal agents. This means that if God is a single independent personal agent, as biblical monotheism demands, he can indeed only enjoy such relations with persons (both human and angelic) beyond himself. It follows that he cannot enjoy loving fellowship 'unless he first create an object for his love'. Of course, this applies to all relational characteristics of God. He can only be a Creator, Sustainer or Redeemer if there is an independent reality beyond himself, which he

---

[54] C.J.F. Williams, 'Neither confounding the persons nor dividing the substance', in Alan Padgett (ed.), *Reason and the Christian Religion* (Oxford, 1994), 238.

[55] Hebblethwaite, *The Incarnation*, 14.

[56] Hebblethwaite, *The Incarnation*, 36, 136, 165.

[57] Hebblethwaite, *The Incarnation*, 134.

creates, sustains or redeems. Does this mean that God's love is not eternal but is only possible after the creation of finite persons beyond himself? Maybe we should respond to this by questioning with St Augustine the legitimacy of speculations about how God was and what God did before the creation of the world.[58] After all, we only have to do with God to the extent that he relates to us, and it is not for us to speculate about how God is or what he does apart from this relationship. As I have argued at length above, faith is an existential and not a speculative enterprise: it has to do with the relationship with God from which our lives and actions derive their meaning and significance and not with speculative theories about how God is or what he does apart from this relationship. From this point of view the important question is not the speculative one whether God's love is eternal in the sense that he has had objects of love from all eternity, but rather the existential one whether his love is eternal in the sense of being always dependable. Since God always remains faithful to his own loving character, we can indeed depend on his eternal love as the basis for our eternal happiness.

---

[58] St Augustine, *Confessions*, 11.12.

PART 4
EPILOGUE

CHAPTER 7

Dialogue and the Matrix of Faith

The Children of Abraham

'Look at Abraham: he put his faith in God, and that faith was counted to him as righteousness. You may take it, then, that it is those who have faith who are Abraham's sons … Thus it is those with faith who share the blessing with faithful Abraham' (Galatians 3:6–7, 9).[1] In the course of history the children of Abraham have diverged into three separate traditions: Judaism, Christianity and Islam. Each of these traditions developed its own ways of understanding the faith of Abraham. Judaism took its point of departure for understanding the faith in Moses and the Torah, Christianity in Jesus and the New Testament, and Islam in Mohammad and the Qu'rān.

Jesus did not think of himself as the founder of a new religion. On the contrary, he was a rabbi who wanted to renew the faith of Israel and not to change it: 'Do not suppose that I have come to abolish the law and the prophets; I did not come to abolish but to complete' (Matthew 5:17). Similarly, Mohammad did not think that he was founding a new religion. He was merely bringing the old faith in the One God to the Arabs who had never had a prophet before and were mostly polytheists. Constantly the Qu'rān points out that Muhammad had not come to deny the Judeo-Christian tradition, to contradict its prophets or start a new religion. He believed that his message was the same as that of Abraham, Moses, David, Solomon or Jesus.[2] He strove to convert the polytheists of Arabia to faith in the One God, but it never occurred to him to require Jews and Christians to be converted to Islam. As far as he was concerned, they were already believers in the One God.[3]

As is often the case with reformers, however, the religious authorities whose tradition Jesus and Mohammad intended to serve, did not accept them. Jesus was rejected by the Jewish establishment of his time and, to his great distress, the Jewish community in Medina refused to accept Mohammad and his message. Contrary to the intention of their founders, Christianity and Islam thus developed in the course of time as distinct religious traditions beside that of the Jews, and were maintained by separate communities of believers. Each of these communities developed their own

---

[1] 'Surely the people standing closest to Abraham are those who follow him, and this Prophet, and those who believe; and God is the Protector of the believers', Sura 2:64.

[2] 'Say you: "We believe in God, and in that which has been sent down on us and sent down on Abraham, Ishmael, Isaac and Jacob, and the Tribes, and that which was given to Moses and Jesus and the Prophets, of their Lord; we make no division between any of them, and to Him we surrender"', Sura 2:130. See also Karin Armstrong, *Islam. A Short History* (London, 2003), 3–20.

[3] 'He sent down upon thee the Book with the truth, confirming what was before it, and he sent down the Torah and the Gospel before, as guidance to the people, and he sent down the Salvation', Sura 3:2.

ways of understanding their faith that were relevant and adequate for the problems
and challenges which they had to face in their separate historical and geographical
circumstances, and intelligible in terms of their own distinct cultural categories of
thought. Thus Judaism remained the exclusive national faith of the Jewish people
and was expressed in the Semitic thought-forms of Israel. Christianity soon
developed into a gentile faith that was expressed in the Hellenistic thought-forms
of the Mediterranean world. Islam addressed itself to the desert tribes of Arabia
and was expressed in Arabian forms of thought. Because of the sociological,
cultural and conceptual differences between these communities of believers,
Judaism, Christianity and Islam tended to drift further and further apart in the course
of time.

There have been occasions in the course of history, such as in medieval Spain
under Moslem rule, when these three communities of believers lived together
amicably and interacted fruitfully. However, these occasions were the exception.
Most of the time they remained in relative isolation from each other and developed
their separate understandings of the faith without much interaction between
them. In an age of globalization, however, such isolation becomes both untenable
and dangerous. Ignorance, misunderstanding and estrangement between these
communities of believers led to conflict, whereas mutual understanding and co-
operation between them can only further the cause of peace in our time. For this
reason it is imperative that the ecumenical dialogue that flourished within the
Christian community of believers in the course of the twentieth century should now
be extended in the twenty-first century to include all three of these communities of
believers. To what extent do Jews, Christians and Moslems not only have shared
origins but also a shared faith, in spite of the real differences that have developed
between them in the course of history?

At this point a serious difficulty arises. Judaism, Christianity and Islam are not
monolithic and unchanging systems of thought that can be compared to each other in
order to determine what beliefs they do and what they do not have in common. They
are *traditions* that have developed, changed and diversified in the course of time. In
many ways the differences *within* each of these traditions are as great as those
between them. I am sure that many Christians who, like myself, have had personal
contacts with Jews or Moslems would have discovered that they have more spiritual
affinity with *some* Jews or Moslems that with *some* Christians! It is difficult enough
to determine which elements of the faith are shared by *all* those who consider
themselves Christians and an impossible task to find elements of the faith that are
shared by *all* Jews, Christians and Moslems! It is, however, plausible to make more
modest claims about which fundamental elements of the faith could reasonably be
defended within the context of all three of these traditions without thereby claiming
that these are held by all Jews, Christians and Moslems.

At the end of Chapter 3 I argued that the view of salvation explained in Chapters 2
and 3 may be understood as the basic structure or matrix of the faith that can be
defended within all three Abrahamic traditions. Thus I consider it plausible to hold

that the following claims could all be defended within the Jewish, Christian and Moslem traditions:

1   Ultimate happiness consists in enjoying that loving fellowship with God in which God makes our ultimate happiness his very own concern and we identify with God by making his will our own and living our lives joyfully in accordance with it.
2   Because of our inability to maintain this loving identification with God consistently, we have become estranged from God and can only regain ultimate happiness by being reconciled with God. The necessary and sufficient conditions for such reconciliation are divine forgiveness as well as repentance and a change of heart by which we can again identify with God's will and live our lives joyfully in accordance with it.
3   In order to attain such a change of heart, it is necessary, first, that God *reveal* himself to us as a loving God who is willing to forgive and also that he should enable us to know what his will for us is. Secondly, it is necessary that he should *create* us as the kind of personal beings who are able to have such fellowship with him and that he should create for us the capacities and opportunities to live our lives in accordance with his will. Thirdly, it is necessary that God should *inspire* our hearts that we should seek his will joyfully out of love and not merely out or duty.

Of course, Jews, Christians and Moslems differ in the metaphors, narratives and doctrines in terms of which they develop and explain this matrix as well as in the forms of spirituality and ritual in terms of which they express it in their lives. However, even within each of these traditions there is no uniformity in the way this common matrix of faith is explained and expressed. In Chapters 4, 5 and 6 I discussed the Christian doctrines of Atonement, Christology and the Trinity as the doctrinal forms in which the matrix of faith has been developed and explained within the Christian tradition. To what extent can my interpretation of these doctrines contribute to a renewed dialogue between the three Abrahamic traditions of faith?

Dialogue and Christian Doctrine

In Chapters 4, 5, and 6 I described the way in which the Fathers tried to interpret the faith in terms of the Platonist forms of thought that were current in the Hellenistic world in which they lived and to which they addressed their message. I argued that these Platonist ways of thinking are so strange to us today, that on their patristic interpretation the doctrines of Atonement, Christology and the Trinity have become puzzling if not unintelligible to most ordinary believers in our time. To this I can now add that the patristic interpretation of these doctrines has made the Christian understanding of the faith even more unpalatable for Jews and Moslems than it would otherwise have been. I have argued that the patristic views on atonement, as well as the substitution theory developed in the twelfth century, entail a view on the divinity of Christ in which Jesus becomes a second divine being distinct from the Father. If by analogy the Holy Spirit is looked on as a third distinct divine being, the result is a social Trinitarianism bordering on tritheism. This is obviously quite incompatible with the monotheism that is a fundamental tenet of both Judaism and Islam. This view of the Trinity amounts to what Ingolf Dalferth calls a 'manifestation of Christian tribalism':

> The doctrine of the Trinity is only an adequate doctrine of God if it is more than a mere expression and manifestation of Christian tribalism. It must be construed to provide an account of *God* – not of a Christian God (whatever that may be) or of some particular beliefs about Father, Son and Spirit which Christians (and not Jews and Moslems) happen to hold over and above their common belief in God. The God of Christian faith is not a particular Christian God but God as experienced by Christians.[4]

To what extent does the Latin version of Trinitarian doctrine that I have defended in Chapter 6 transcend such 'Christian tribalism' and provide a more satisfactory point of departure for dialogue with Jews and Moslems? The view that I have proposed is thoroughly monotheistic and to that extent not at odds with Judaism and Islam. God is a single personal being who desires our loving fellowship and acts in three ways in order to make such fellowship possible. As Father he *creates* us and grants us the abilities and the opportunities to identify with him in love. In Jesus the Son he *reveals* to us both himself as a loving God who desires our fellowship as well as what it means to live a life of fellowship according to his will. In this sense Jesus is both 'very God' and 'very man'. Through his Spirit God *enlightens* our minds and *inspires* our hearts that we may know and love him and thus find our ultimate happiness in his fellowship. In all this, Father, Son and Spirit are not three divine agents but three forms of agency exercised by one and the same divine agent who is God.

To what extent might Jews and Moslems recognize their own faith in this view of the triune agency of God? The claim that God is our Creator and that his Spirit enlightens and inspires us, should present no problems within either the Jewish or the Islamic traditions. Jews and Moslems should also have no difficulty in accepting the claim that God should reveal himself and his will to us if we are to be reconciled with him and enjoy his fellowship. The difficulty lies with the Christian claim that it is in Jesus as the Christ that God reveals this to us. For the Jews, Christ was a stumbling block from the very beginning. For them it was offensive to claim that the power and the wisdom of God is revealed to us in the cross of Christ (see 1 Corinthians 1:23–4). This offensiveness has been compounded by the fact that for Jews, Jesus has become the symbol of 2000 years of persecution by Christians who held the Jews responsible for the crucifixion. C.A. Lamb points out that

---

4 Ingolf Dalferth, 'The eschatological roots of the doctrine of the Trinity', in Christoph Schwöbel (ed.), *Trinitarian Theology Today* (Edinburgh, 1995), 155–6.

among Jews the person of Jesus became an acute embarrassment, and a long tradition going back to the Talmud will only refer to him as 'That Man' (ha-ish ha-uw). His name was altered in Hebrew from Yeshua to Yeshu, which was taken to mean one whose name was to be blotted out as accursed.[5]

However, Lamb goes on to quote a number of recent Jewish scholars (Martin Buber, Leo Beck, Franz Rosenzweig and Pinchas Lapide) who view Jesus as an exemplary Jewish personality with whom they can identify. However, this does not mean that they accept the claim that Jesus is the revelation of 'very God and very man'.

While Jesus is an embarrassment for the Jews, he is a highly honoured and venerated prophet for Moslems.[6] In some ways he is even more venerable than Mohammad. Thus, according to the Qu'rān, he was born of the Virgin Mary and unlike Mohammad he is called the Messiah and even described as the 'word of God' and as 'a spirit from God' (Sura 4:171). However, the claim that he is the Son of God is resolutely rejected since this is too much like Apollo being the son of Zeus and that would contradict the monotheistic claims of Islam. Jesus is the messenger of God but not a God himself. God is one and there are no Gods beside him. From a Christian point of view, the most startling claim about Jesus in the Qu'rān is the denial of his crucifixion (Sura 4:157–9). Here it is stated that the Jews mistakenly claim that they had crucified 'the Messiah, Jesus son of Mary, the messenger of God'. God prevented this from happening by 'taking him up unto himself' and letting the Jews crucify someone else (Judas or Jesus Barabbas) in his place. This view is reminiscent of that of the Frankish king Clovis (465–511) who is claimed to have said of the crucifixion: 'If I and my Franks had been there it would never have happened'! Denying the crucifixion in this way entails the denial of the role that Christians claim the crucifixion plays in our salvation. Moslems therefore cannot share the view that it is in Jesus and in his crucifixion that we come to know the compassionate love of God and the price of forgiveness which he is willing to pay for us to be reconciled with him.

Exclusivism

For Christians, then, it is in the cross of Christ that we come to know the compassionate love of God. Sometimes this claim is extended to assert that it is *only* through the cross of Christ that this can be known. Thus, for example, the commission on faith of the United Church of Canada declared that 'without the particular knowledge of God in Jesus Christ, men do not really know God at all'.[7] This entails

---

[5] C.A. Lamb, *Jesus through Other Eyes: Christology in Multi-faith Context* (Oxford, 1982), 26. Chapter 3 discusses the attitudes to Jesus in Judaism.

[6] On the Moslem view of Jesus, see chapter 1 of Lamb, *Jesus through Other Eyes* and chapter 8 of Anton Wessels, *Islam in Stories* (Leuven, 2002).

[7] Quoted by Wilfred Cantwell Smith in 'The Christian in a religiously plural world', in John Hick and Brian Hebblethwaite, *Christianity and Other Religions* (Glasgow, 1980), 98.

that Jews and Moslems, together with adherents of all other faiths who do not accept Jesus as the Christ, do not 'really know God'. From a Christian point of view this claim is preposterous. Of course Christians claim that Christ is the incarnation of the Word of God. But this is the same Word that was already revealed in the Torah. Thus Christians would never claim that the people of Israel in the Old Testament did not 'really know God'! In fact, John Calvin asserts 'that in the Christian Church scarcely one is to be found who, in excellence of faith, can be compared to Abraham, and that the Prophets were so distinguished by the power of the Spirit, that even in the present day they give light to the whole world'.[8] Thus, in the light of their faith the prophets could witness to the compassionate love of God in their own lives and experience. Wiles points out that 'it does not seem too fanciful to claim that it was the pain of Hosea's continuing love for his unfaithful wife which gave rise to the distinctive emphasis in his oracles on the compassionate love of Yahweh for his erring and suffering people'.[9] Clearly, then, Christians cannot claim that Jews who did not know or do not accept the revelation of God in Jesus, do not 'really know God'. Similarly it would be absurd for Christians to claim that Moslems who do not believe in the crucifixion of Christ do not 'really know God' and are ignorant of his compassionate love. In fact every sura of the Qu'rān is prefaced by the words: 'In the Name of God, the Merciful, the Compassionate'.

Wilfred Cantwell Smith extends this claim to include adherents of other faiths beyond the Abrahamic traditions. Here he makes what he calls an 'empirical observation':

> The evidence would seem overwhelming that in fact individual Buddhists, Hindus, Moslems and others have known, and in fact do know, God. I personally have friends from these communities whom it seems to me preposterous to think about in any other way. (If we do not have friends among these communities, we should probably refrain from generalizations about them.)[10]

These words of Smith give rise to three comments. First, we could agree with Smith that God in his almighty wisdom is able to make himself known in many ways, also to those who adhere to faiths other than Christianity and also beyond the Abrahamic traditions:

> The God whom we have come to know ... reaches out after all men everywhere, and speaks to all who will listen. Both within and without the Church men listen all too dimly. Yet both within and without the church, so far as we can see, God does somehow enter into men's hearts.[11]

Similarly Jews and Moslems should admit that they too do not have a privileged access to the knowledge of God. We should all come to see that others outside our

---

[8] John Calvin, *The Institutes of the Christian Religion*, trans. Henry Beveridge (London, 1953), 2.11.6.

[9] Maurice Wiles, *The Remaking of Christian Doctrine* (London, 1974), 71.

[10] Smith, 'Religiously plural world', 102.

[11] Smith, 'Religiously plural world', 107.

own tradition, and especially those who adhere to the other Abrahamic traditions, can also come to know the God whom we have come to know through our own tradition.

Secondly, Smith's claim that his friends in other faiths 'really know God' refers to knowledge of the heart and not merely of the mind. We can only 'really know God' to the extent that we have fellowship with God and achieve a 'union of wills' with God, and this, for Christians, will manifest itself in the Christ-like character of our lives. Knowing God is leaving what St Bernard calls the land of unlikeness and returning to the land of likeness where our lives become like that of Christ and we do not merely know *about* the compassionate love of God but also, like Christ, share this love by manifesting it in our relations with others. Jews and Moslems accept other paradigms of the compassionate love of God than Christians do. Nevertheless it is also true for them that knowing God is a knowledge of the heart and not merely of the mind. It remains true for all of us that knowing God is not merely knowing *about* his compassionate love but sharing this love by manifesting in it our relations with others both inside and outside our own traditions. The claims of Jews, Christians and Moslems that they know God becomes a hollow and blasphemous claim if they do not show God's compassionate love in their lives but rather do terrible things to others in his name!

Thirdly, Smith's claim about his friends in other religious communities knowing God in this sense can hardly be called an 'empirical observation'. It is far rather a claim that he makes in the light of his own Christian faith. It is only possible in the light of our knowledge of God as revealed in Christ, for us to discern that others (and ourselves) inside and outside the church can be said to 'really know God' in a Christ-like way. In this sense Christians have to claim that the revelation of God's love in Christ is *paradigmatic* since it is only in the light of God's self-revelation in Jesus Christ that we can say what it means to 'know God' and be reconciled with him. Thus Smith has to admit that 'because God is what he is, because he is what Christ has shown him to be, *therefore* other men *do* live in his presence. Also, therefore, we (as Christians) know this to be so.'[12]

It is therefore in the light of the paradigm of Christ that Christians may come to discern their own faith in that of Jews and Moslems. This also applies to Jews and Moslems even though they accept different paradigms for their faith. Thus for Jews the Torah is the paradigm of their faith and for Moslems the Qu'rān. Whereas for Christians the Word of God is incarnate in Jesus Christ, for Jews this is so in the Torah and for Moslems in the Qu'rān. In spite of the fact that these three traditions have different paradigms of faith, these different paradigms may yet enable them to discern the faith of their common father, Abraham, in each other and thus together seek their ultimate happiness in the loving fellowship of Abraham's God.

---

12 Smith, 'Religiously plural world', 106.

Index